Twentieth Edition

2021 & 2022
NIRSA Flag & Touch
Football Rules Book &
Officials' Manual

Leaders in Collegiate Recreation
www.nirsa.org

HUMAN KINETICS

ISBN: 978-1-7182-0811-7 (print)

Reprinted with permission of the National Federation of State High School Associations.

Thanks to BSN SPORTS for the flag belts used in the cover photo. Contact Chris Hutton at 800-527-7510, x9046, to purchase flag belts.

The web addresses cited in this text were current as of February 2021, unless otherwise noted.

Senior Acquisitions Editor: Amy N. Tocco; **Managing Editor:** Derek Campbell; **Copyeditor:** Karla Walsh; **Permissions Manager:** Dalene Reeder; **Graphic Designer:** Denise Lowry; **Cover Designer:** Keri Evans; **Cover Design Specialist:** Susan Rothermel Allen; **Photograph (cover):** Human Kinetics; **Photo Production Manager:** Jason Allen; **Senior Art Manager:** Kelly Hendren; **Illustrations:** © Human Kinetics, unless otherwise noted; **Printer:** Versa Press

Printed in the United States of America   10 9 8 7 6 5 4 3 2 1

The paper in this book is certified under a sustainable forestry program.

Human Kinetics
1607 N. Market Street
Champaign, IL 61820
USA

United States and International
Website: **US.HumanKinetics.com**
Email: info@hkusa.com
Phone: 1-800-747-4457

Canada
Website: **Canada.HumanKinetics.com**
Email: info@hkcanada.com

NIRSA
www.nirsa.org
541-766-8211

E8386

Tell us what you think!
Human Kinetics would love to hear what we can do to improve the customer experience. Use this QR code to take our brief survey.

CONTENTS

*Any rule and play interpretation not discussed in this rules book is governed by the National Federation of State High School Associations' *Football Rules Book* and *Football Case Book*.

NIRSA: LEADERS IN COLLEGIATE RECREATION

NIRSA is the premier association of leaders in collegiate recreation that transforms lives and facilitates the development of healthy communities worldwide. By providing opportunities for learning and growth, supporting and sharing meaningful research, and fostering networking among our member community, NIRSA is a leader in higher education and champion for the advancement of recreation, sport, and wellness. Since its founding in 1950, NIRSA membership has grown to comprise nearly 4,500 dedicated professionals, students, and associates, serving an estimated 8.1 million students. Supported by the NIRSA Headquarters team, based in Corvallis, Oregon, NIRSA is governed by volunteer leaders from across North America.

NIRSA provides access to educational resource materials as well as a professional support network. Ensuring that those involved in recreational sports remain current and up-to-date is a prime concern for NIRSA. Through professional support materials and sponsored projects, the quality of collegiate recreation is greatly enhanced. NIRSA publications, career opportunities services, the NIRSA Championship Series, and sponsored national and regional conferences and workshops contribute to the overall quality of collegiate recreation programs, services, and personnel.

The 11 small-college intramural directors who originally met as the founding members of the association could not have imagined the rapid and extensive growth of the collegiate recreation field. As the field has evolved, so has NIRSA. Today, the challenges of meeting the recreational sports programming needs of over 2,200 colleges, universities, military installations, and local communities are met by highly trained and caring professionals supported through the efforts of NIRSA.

STATEMENT ON SOCIAL JUSTICE

The Flag & Touch Football Editorial Board supports the NIRSA Championship Series Code of Conduct and NIRSA's Statement for Equity, Diversity, and Inclusion as a standard for how individuals should act during all Championship Series events.

The Editorial Board rejects behaviors that are abusive or derogatory, including the use of verbal and nonverbal profanity, disrespectful language, obscene gestures, bullying, and homophobic or transphobic expressions. We reject any form of prejudice or discrimination on the basis of age; ability; ethnicity; sex; gender, gender identity, or gender expression; heritage; language; national origin; race; religion; sexual orientation; or socioeconomic status. Instead, we acknowledge and respect our unique identities and affirm our common humanity. Finally, we embrace the position that, in order for proper sporting behavior to prevail, players, coaches, officials, and spectators must display respect, fairness, civility, honesty, and responsibility before, during, and after competition.

The Editorial Board seeks to advance the game of flag football in a manner that best serves participants of all identities and backgrounds. We believe the sport of flag football unifies participants around the world by creating stronger communities grounded in mutual respect, antiracism, and continuous efforts towards inclusion.

NIRSA FLAG & TOUCH FOOTBALL EDITORIAL BOARD

DEDICATION: ZACH GILBERT

In 1987, NIRSA began a tradition of dedicating each edition of the NIRSA Flag & Touch Football Rules Book & Officials' Manual to a person who has made significant contributions and played a pivotal role in the development of flag football. The honoree for the dedication of this twentieth edition of the book is Zach Gilbert.

A NIRSA member since 2002, Zach has served our game in countless roles. Not only has he dedicated his time to advancing the sport at the state, regional, and national levels, but he has also served in a variety of capacities outside NIRSA tournament events.

He began officiating as an undergraduate student at the University of Arkansas. During that time, he worked at the national tournament for four consecutive years (2000 through 2003) and was recognized as an All-American official twice, in 2002 and 2003. Following his time on the field, Zach remained connected to the sport of flag football through his committee and clinician experience. He volunteered for NIRSA's Sports Officials' Development Program, serving on the Flag Football Rules Committee from 2009 to 2015, which included an appointment as the chair for the 2011-2012 cycle. Since 2004, Zach has attended the NIRSA national tournament as an evaluator and clinician every year. At the state and regional levels, Zach has a wealth of experience as an officials' and tournament director, and he continues to contribute to flag football events each season.

Zach has extensive experience on the field, but he is also committed to serving the game through educational opportunities, such as clinics and workshops. Since 2016, he has assisted with a flag football officials' clinic at a U.S. Army installation (Fort Jackson). He led a flag football preconference workshop for the 2005 annual conference. He presented three other times at an annual conference, in 2003, 2011, and 2014; his presentations focused on flag football officiating ("A Guide to Decide: Officiating Unsportsmanlike Behavior"), officials' evaluations ("Lights! Camera! Evaluate! Integrating Video Evaluations Into a Sports Officials' Development Program"), and tournament administration ("Behind the Action: Planning and Assessing Events").

For two decades, Zach has remained connected to the sport of flag football as well as to the rules book and officials' manual. He studied and applied the rules and mechanics as an official, advanced and shaped the game during his time on the rules committee, and continues to promote and share the game through his volunteerism for events within and outside NIRSA. His experience has allowed him to contribute numerous suggestions for rules and mechanics changes over the years. Zach's experience as an official, evaluator, and educator is second to none, but what makes him stand out are the energy with which leads, his passion for football, and his commitment to student development through officiating.

NIRSA: Leaders in Collegiate Recreation proudly recognizes Zach Gilbert for his outstanding contributions to NIRSA flag and touch football by dedicating this publication in his honor.

PAST DEDICATION RECIPIENTS

1987 & 1988 **Dr. Rodney J. Grambeau,** University of Michigan
1989 & 1990 **Dr. Louis M. Marciani,** East Stroudsburg University
James L. "Jet" Smith, University of New Orleans
1991 & 1992 **Stephen Rey,** University of Southern Mississippi
1993 & 1994 **Jim Potter,** Trinity University
1995 & 1996 **Earl Birdy,** Carnegie Mellon University
1997 & 1998 **Will M. Holsberry,** NIRSA
1999 & 2000 **Dr. Bruce L. Maurer,** The Ohio State University
2001 & 2002 **Bob Gildersleeve,** Grand Valley State University
2003 & 2004 **Gary E. Albright,** Arkansas State University
2005 & 2006 **David Gaskins,** East Carolina University
2007 & 2008 **The University of New Orleans**
2009 & 2010 **Bradley Petty,** Angelo State University
2011 & 2012 **Kurt Klier,** University of Maryland
2013 & 2014 **David Parker,** University of North Carolina-Wilmington
2015 & 2016 **Mary Callender,** NIRSA
2017 & 2018 **Ken "Murphy" Whitman,** University of New Orleans
2019 & 2020 **James L. Leonard,** Department of Army-Europe MWR

MOVING CLOSER TO A STANDARDIZED FOOTBALL CODE

The NIRSA Flag & Touch Football Rules Committee was created 40 years ago and charged with the responsibility of developing a standardized code of rules, interpretations, and officials' mechanics. Unlike most other intramural sports, there was no nationally recognized set of flag and touch football rules.

Prior to developing rule proposals in 1982, the committee first reviewed the literature related to flag and touch football. They decided to conduct several national research[1] projects concerning injury frequencies as related to the rules. In addition, many of the nation's colleges and universities were surveyed to determine which rules and interpretations were being administered. The results of these massive research projects played an integral role during those early decision-making processes.

The nineteen editions of the *NIRSA Flag & Touch Football Rules Book & Officials' Manual* have been very successful. These rules are used by thousands of colleges, universities, recreation departments, high schools, correctional institutions, military installations, YMCAs and YWCAs, the Department of Army–Europe, and the Department of the Navy.

In 2014, the NIRSA Board of Directors approved the Flag & Touch Football Editorial Board. The 12-member board formalizes the process for reviewing, editing, and publishing the rules and officials' manual. The *NIRSA Rules Book and Officials' Manual* is revised biannually. The Editorial Board seeks and needs input, which can be submitted through the NIRSA website. After all, these are *your* rules and mechanics.

The twentieth edition of the *NIRSA Flag & Touch Football Rules Book & Officials' Manual* is a culmination of this effort. It is a continuing effort by the NIRSA membership to standardize the rules and mechanics for this great game.

---

[1] Participating colleges and universities included Georgia Institute of Technology, Illinois State University, Indiana University, The Ohio State University, Trinity University, University of California at Los Angeles, University of Illinois, University of Maryland, University of New Orleans, University of Southern Mississippi, University of Tennessee, and Washington State University.

Valuable Programming Tools for the Flag and Touch Football Administrator

The *NIRSA Rules Book and Officials' Manual* is an excellent start for the sports administrator placed in charge of a flag or touch football program at a college, university, military installation, high school, community recreation agency, correctional institution, or YMCA/YWCA.

Acknowledgments

NIRSA acknowledges the following for their outstanding contributions to the *NIRSA Rules Book and Officials' Manual*.

> Department of Army–Europe, IMCOM-E Support and Officials
> Department of the Navy, Management, Officials, and Players
> Bruce Maurer, The Ohio State University, Past Editor
> Jim Potter, Trinity University, Past Editor of the *Officials' Manual*
> National, Regional, and State Flag Football Championships
> Florida High School Athletic Association
> Players, Officials, and Contributors

NIRSA Headquarters is located at 4185 SW Research Way, Corvallis, OR 97333, (541) 766-8211.

Leaders in Collegiate Recreation

www.nirsa.org

OFFICIAL NIRSA RULES AND INTERPRETATIONS FOR FLAG & TOUCH FOOTBALL

Interpretations for flag and touch football are integrated into the NIRSA Rules Book. Specialized flag and co-rec rules have been printed utilizing **bold type**.

If there is a conflict between the Official Rules and the Rule Interpretations, the Official Rules take precedence.

Flag rules are identified by utilizing the illustrated flag belt.

An official's signal (S) refers to the NIRSA Official Flag Football Signals located on pages 117-118.

Changes for the twentieth edition are identified in the rules by a shaded background.

The Rule Interpretations are dedicated to the hundreds of thousands of intramural football officials who have given so unselfishly to the great game of flag and touch football over the years. Their enthusiasm, insight, rules knowledge, courage, and sense of purpose have helped make this book possible.

Please contact the Editorial Board for any interpretations of rules or play situations: http://play.nirsa.net/flag-football/

CHANGES FOR 2021 AND 2022

The *NIRSA Rules Book and Officials' Manual* takes priority over materials listed below.

Rules Book

1-2-3 **30-Yard Lines.** The 3, 10, and 30 yard lines shall be marked with a line 2 yards wide and 4" thick. Adding the 30 yard lines provides a visual reference point on the field for restarting play after a safety and penalty enforcement.

2-6 **Field Areas.** Added definitions for the following areas: The Field, Field of Play, Side Zones, End Zones, and Restricted Area.

7-2-4 **Disconcerting Act.** No defensive player shall use disconcerting acts or words prior to the snap in an attempt to interfere with A's signals (S7 and S23).

8-3-1 **2 Minute Warning.** If a team is ahead by 19 or more points when the Referee announces the 2 minute warning for the 4th period, the game shall be over. Prior to implementing the Mercy Rule, the Referee shall apply the Extension of Period Rule (3-2-1). NOTE: Game clock starts according to Rule 3.

8-3-2 **After 2 Minute Warning.** If a team scores during the last 2 minutes of the 4th period and that score creates a point differential of 19 or more points, the game shall end at that point.

8-5 **Touchdown Values.** All touchdowns are 6 points.

8-8-1D **Safety Value: 2 Points.** After a safety, the ball shall be snapped by the scoring team at their own 30 yard line, unless moved by penalty.

9-1-1 **Noncontact Acts.** Added "Intentionally kicking at the ball" as an illegal noncontact act. Removed "Using words similar to the offensive audibles and quarterback cadence prior to the snap in an attempt to interfere with A's signals or movements" from the list of illegal noncontact acts.

9-3-3 **Screen Blocking.** An offensive screen block may occur anywhere on the field and shall take place without contact. The screen blocker shall have their hands and arms at their sides or behind their back when screen blocking. Any use of the hands, arms, elbows, legs, or body to initiate contact that displaces an opponent during a screen block is illegal. A blocker may use their hand(s) or arm(s) to break a fall or retain their balance.

9-3-4 **Screen Blocking Fundamentals.** A player who screens shall not do any of the following: (A) initiate contact when blocking a stationary opponent from any direction; (B) prevent an opponent from avoiding contact by (1) taking a position closer than a normal step when behind a stationary opponent or (2) taking a position within 1 or 2 steps of a moving opponent, so that the opponent cannot stop or change direction before contact; or (C) after taking a legal position, move to maintain it, unless the screener moves in the same direction and path as the opponent. If a screener violates any of these provisions and contact results, they have committed a foul.

9-3-5 **Interlocked Blocking.** Teammates of a runner or passer may legally screen block, but they shall not use interlocked blocking, such as grasping a teammate or encircling an opponent in any manner.

4 on 4 Football Rules Summary

7-5-1   **Runner.** An A runner cannot advance the ball through the A scrimmage line (1st ball spotter-orange). There are no restrictions: (A) once the ball has been touched by any player beyond the A scrimmage line, (B) after a change of team possession, or (C) after a legal forward pass. *Penalty:* Illegal Advancement, 3 yards from the previous spot (S19).

7-7-1   **Legal Forward Pass.** There must be a legal forward pass each down. A has 5 seconds to release the ball on a forward pass. If A fails to release the ball in time, it is a loss of down and the ball is next snapped at the previous spot. The Referee will sound their whistle at 5 seconds if the passer has possession of the football.

Officials' Mechanics and Manual

3-7-1   **Eligible Substitutions.** Clarifies the signal to be used when reporting an illegal substitution foul.

7-7-2   **Illegal Forward Pass.** Clarifies the signals to be used when reporting an illegal forward pass foul.

Flag and Touch Football Fundamentals

I. Possession
1. A live ball is always in the possession of a team.
2. A live ball is in player possession or is loose.
3. A loose ball is in the possession of the team whose player was last in possession.
4. A player in possession of a live ball is a runner.
5. A player cannot fumble before gaining possession. Once a fumble, muff, or backward pass touches the ground, it is dead.
6. No foul causes loss of the ball.
7. After a distance penalty, the ball belongs to the team that was in possession at the time of the foul according to applicable rules. Team possession may then change if a new series is awarded.
8. Possession of a live ball in the opponent's end zone is always a touchdown.

II. Downs and the Zone Line-to-Gain
1. A down begins when the ball becomes live and ends when it becomes dead.
2. Whether the next down will be 1st is determined at the time the ball becomes dead and after considering the effect of any act, except a nonplayer foul or unsportsmanlike conduct, that occurred during the down.
3. If Team R is first to touch a punt beyond K's scrimmage line, a new series will be awarded to the team in possession at end of the down, unless there was a foul before the punt and the penalty was accepted, or there was a double foul, or there was an inadvertent whistle during the punt following the touching by Team R.
4. The only defensive fouls that automatically cause a 1st down are Roughing the Passer and Illegally Tampering with the Flag Belt.
5. If the penalty is accepted for a live ball foul by either team during a down in which time expires, the period must be extended by an untimed down. The exceptions are unsportsmanlike fouls, nonplayer fouls, fouls that specify a loss of down, or fouls as specified in 3-2-3A.
6. No series can ever start on a down other than 1st.
7. The zone line-to-gain is established when the referee blows the ready for play whistle on 1st down of a new series for Team A. The zone line-to-gain will be the 20, 40, or goal line closest to Team A's scrimmage line in the direction of Team B's end zone. During overtime, however, the zone line-to-gain will always be the goal line.

III. Dead Ball
1. A game official's whistle seldom kills the play. The ball is already dead by Rule.
2. No live ball foul causes the ball to become dead.
3. A dead ball may become live only by a legal snap.
4. Catching is always preceded by touching of the ball; thus, if touching causes the ball to become dead, securing possession of the ball has no significance.

IV. Punts

1. For Team K to legally punt the ball, Team K has to declare a punt prior to the ready for play. Team K may punt the ball only once per down.
2. A punt always ends as soon as any player secures possession.
3. Any Team R player may catch or recover a punt in the field of play and advance. All muffs by Team R that strike the ground are dead at the spot where the ball touches the ground.
4. Any fair catch signal will be ignored by the players and officials—the ball remains live.
5. A punt becomes dead when it breaks the plane of Team R's goal line and is a touchback.
6. Punts may be legally batted in the following manner: Team R may block the ball: (a) once it has been punted, and Team K may bat an airborne or grounded punt beyond their scrimmage line toward their own goal line; or (b) if a punt in flight beyond the neutral zone is batted by Team K toward its own goal line when no Team R player is in position to catch the ball.
7. First touching of a punt by Team K is ignored if the penalty is accepted for a foul during the down.

V. Passes

1. All players are considered eligible receivers.
2. Team A may throw one forward pass per down.
3. A handed ball is not a pass.
4. Any pass in flight may be batted in any direction by an eligible receiver unless it is a backward pass batted forward by the passing team.
5. A forward pass interference foul can occur only beyond A's scrimmage line.

VI. Screen Blocking and Deflagging/Tagging

1. Blocking other than screen blocking by either team is not permissible.
2. Using hands, arms, elbows, legs, or body to block or displace an opponent is illegal.
3. A player in possession of a live ball is considered deflagged once their flag belt has been removed legally by an opponent. No player may remove their flag belt or the flag belt of an opponent not in possession of a live ball.
4. Players in possession of the ball without a flag belt must be tagged with 1 hand between the shoulder and knees.
5. No player may tackle the runner by grasping or encircling with the hand(s) or arm(s) and taking the opponent toward the ground as in tackle football.

VII. Fouls

1. No live ball foul causes the covering official to sound their whistle immediately.
2. A live ball foul cannot be paired with a dead ball foul to create a double or multiple foul.
3. A double foul results only when both teams commit fouls—other than nonplayer fouls or unsportsmanlike conduct—during the same live ball period, or if team possession changed during the down and the foul by the team in final possession was prior to the change, or if there were a change of possession and the team in final possession accepted the penalty for its opponent's foul.
4. While it is possible to have several running plays during a down, there can only be one loose ball play during a down.

VIII. Penalty Measurement

1. The distance penalty for any foul *may* be declined.
2. Penalties are either 5 or 10 yards.
3. Penalties are given according to the All-But-One Enforcement Principle for any live ball foul except the following:
   a. Fouls that occur simultaneously with the snap
   b. A foul by the opponents of the scoring team during a successful Try or touchdown when the score is accepted
   c. A nonplayer foul or unsportsmanlike conduct
   d. Roughing the Passer when the dead ball spot is beyond the neutral zone and there has been no change of team possession
   e. Kick Catching Interference when the offended team accepts a penalty of 10 yards from the spot of the foul
   f. Fouls by the kicking team during a punt play when the receiving team elects to have the penalty enforced from the dead ball spot
4. Penalty enforcement for any dead ball foul, nonplayer foul, or unsportsmanlike conduct is from the succeeding spot unless the foul occurs on a scoring play and the scoring team chooses enforcement at the succeeding spot (14 yard line or 10 yard line in overtime).
5. The penalty for any one of the 5 illegal passes is a loss of 5 yards, and the down is counted, except for a forward pass following change of team possession.
6. No penalty directly results in a safety. However, if a distance penalty is enforced from behind the offender's goal line toward their end line, it is a safety.
7. The penalty for a live ball foul by the defensive team is administered from the basic spot, except when that spot is in the end zone.
8. The loss of down aspect of a penalty has no significance following a change of possession or if the line-to-gain is reached after enforcement.

IX. Co-Rec

1. A Team A runner who is a man may not advance the ball through the Team A scrimmage line unless the ball has been touched beyond the Team A or K scrimmage line or after a legal forward pass.
2. A legal forward pass completion from a man to a man makes the next play closed. The play remains closed until: (a) there is a legal forward pass completion involving a woman who is a passer or receiver, and (b) the play gains positive yardage. This also applies to the Try.
3. Team A cannot have two consecutive man-to-man forward pass completions. (Illegal Reception carries a loss of down, and the play remains closed.) This also applies to the Try. A legal forward pass caught jointly by teammates, one of whom is a man and one of whom is a woman, is considered a reception by a woman.
4. All fouls other than a foul for Illegal Reception, whether accepted or declined, shall have no effect on whether the next play is open or closed.

X. If in Doubt . . .

1. Continue the game (Rule 1).
2. Consider the safety of all participants to be paramount to the game (Rules 1 and 3).
3. It is not a catch (Rule 2).
4. It is not a foul (Rule 2).
5. Enforce Illegally Consuming Time (Rule 3).
6. A snap close to the ground remains live (Rule 4).
7. The flag belt has been pulled (Rule 4).
8. The ball is released (Rule 4).
9. The out-of-bounds punt is short of the zone line-to-gain (Rule 5).
10. The A player first touched the snap 2 yards behind A's scrimmage line (Rule 7).
11. The pass is backward (Rule 7).
12. The passer is behind A's scrimmage line (Rule 7).
13. The pass is legal (Rule 7).
14. It is a touchback (Rule 8).
15. The out-of-bounds punt near the goal line is a touchback (Rule 8).

RULE 1. THE GAME, FIELD, PLAYERS, AND EQUIPMENT

Section 1. General Provisions

Article 1. Object of the Game.

It is the object of the game for 1 team to carry or pass the ball across the opponent's goal line. The game is won by the team that accumulates the most points.

Article 2. The Game.

The game shall be played between 2 teams of 7 players each. Four players are required to start the game and avoid a forfeit. The game may be continued with fewer than 4 players as long as the team has a chance to win. NOTE: If in doubt, continue the game.

Article 3. The Co-Rec Game.

The co-rec game shall be played between 2 teams of 8 players, 4 men and 4 women. Teams with 7 players shall be 4 men and 3 women or 4 women and 3 men. Teams with 6 players shall be 3 men and 3 women, 4 men and 2 women, or 4 women and 2 men. Teams with 5 players, 3 men and 2 women or 2 men and 3 women, are required to start the game and avoid a forfeit. The game may be continued with fewer than 5 players as long as the team has a chance to win. NOTE: If in doubt, continue the game.

NOTE: Member institutions are encouraged to adopt and use the NIRSA Transgender Athlete Participation Policy for their events (see play.nirsa.net/nirsa-championship-series/player-eligibility-requirements). This policy is mandatory for NIRSA Championship Series events.

Article 4. Supervision.

The game shall be played under the supervision of 2 to 4 officials. The officials are Referee, Back Judge, Line Judge, and Field Judge. It is recommended strongly that a minimum of 3 officials be used. Positions and responsibilities are found in the *Officials' Manual*.

Article 5. Captains.

Each coach or player-coach shall designate to the Referee the captain(s). If more than 1 player is designated, a speaking captain must be selected to make all decisions.

Article 6. Persons Subject to the Rules.

Players, nonplayers, and spectators affiliated with the team are subject to the Rules of the game and shall be governed by decisions of officials assigned to the game.

Article 7. Referee's Authority.

The Referee shall have authority to rule promptly, and in the spirit of good sporting behavior, on any situation not specifically covered in the Rules. The Referee's decisions are final in all matters pertaining to the game.

Article 8. Officials' Authority.

The officials shall assume authority for the contest 30 minutes prior to the scheduled game time, or as soon as they arrive. The officials' jurisdiction extends through the Referee's declaration of the end of the 4th period or overtime.

Section 2. The Field

Article 1. Safety Margin.

No hard and unyielding rigid fixtures (e.g., trees, poles, fences) shall be located within 5 yards of the sidelines or 10 yards of the end lines, unless covered with at least 1/2" of closed-cell, slow-recovery rubber or other material of the same minimum thickness and having similar physical properties. NOTE: If in doubt, consider the safety of all participants to be paramount to the game.

Article 2. Adjacent Fields.

When fields are located in close proximity, there shall be a minimum of 5 yards between "side by side" fields and 10 yards between "end on end" fields.

Article 3. Field Markings.

The width of the field shall be lined at 20 yard intervals from goal line to goal line. These zone markings may be changed according to field dimensions. All yard lines inside the boundaries shall stop 4" from each sideline. There shall be 2 hash marks. They shall run parallel with each sideline, located 15 yards "in" from each sideline. The 3 and 10 yard Try lines and the 30 yard lines shall be 2 yards wide and 4" thick. Both 14 yard lines shall be marked with an "X" and shall have a height of 1 yard and a line thickness of 4". White is the recommended color for all field markings.

Article 4. Facility Limitations.

In case of facility limitations, distances of field length and width can be modified. However, end zone length must *always* be 10 yards. If the field length is modified, shorten all 4 zones equally so they are the same length. NOTE: When zones are shortened, the 3 and 10 yard Try lines remain the same. The 14 yard lines must be located 6 yards from the nearest zone line. The 30 yard lines must each be located 10 yards from the 40 yard line.

Article 5. Goal Line.

The entire width of each goal line shall be a part of the end zone.

Article 6. Team Box.

On each side of the field a team box shall be designated for the players and nonplayers. This team box is located 2 yards off the sideline and between the 20 yard lines. When the playing area is modified, so shall be the team box. If teams cannot agree on a sideline, the Referee shall conduct a coin toss. Both team boxes may be located on the same side of the field, provided each team box is marked between their respective 20 and 35 yard lines.

Article 7. End Zone Pylons.

Twelve soft, flexible pylons shall be placed at the inside corner of the intersections of the sideline with the goal lines and the end lines, and at the intersections of the end lines and hash marks extended. The 4 pylons located at the hash marks extended shall be positioned 3' beyond the end line.

Article 8. Sideline Zone Line-to-Gain Markers.

20 yard line and 40 yard line markers, constructed of soft and pliable materials, shall be located 6' beyond the sideline.

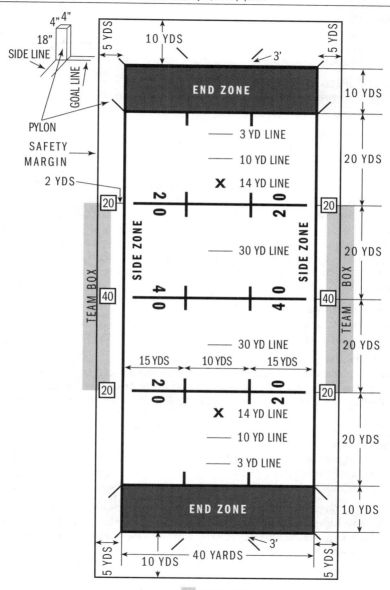

TEAM BOX

Article 9. Field Numbers and Hash Marks.

White field yard line numbers shall be 6' in height and 4' in width, with the tops of the numbers 5 yards from the sidelines, if used. Hash marks shall be 6' long and 4" wide, and intersect with the 20 and 40 yard lines. Additional hash marks, 3' long and 4" wide, shall touch the goal line and extend into the field of play.

Article 10. Field Orientation.

It is highly recommended that fields be laid out in a north/south orientation when new facilities are planned.

Article 11. Field Slope.

It is recommended there be a slope of 1/4" per foot from the center of the field to each sideline on a natural grass field.

Section 3. Game Equipment

Article 1. The Ball.

The official ball shall be pebble-grained leather or rubber covered and meet the recommendations of size and shape for a regulation football. There are no requirements regarding ball pressure and markings. Games involving only men shall use the regular size ball. The regular, intermediate, youth, or junior size football shall be used for all other games. The Referee shall be the sole judge of any ball offered for play and may change the ball during play at his or her discretion. During the game, each team shall use a legal ball of its choice when in possession.

Article 2. Ball Spotters.

2 soft and pliable ball spotters shall be used. 1, orange in color, shall mark A's scrimmage line. The 2nd, gold in color, shall mark B's scrimmage line. The ball spotters shall always be 1 yard apart.

Article 3. Down Box.

A down box shall be used to indicate the number of the down and placed at the zone line-to-gain. It shall be positioned 2 yards out of bounds and operated under the jurisdiction of the Line Judge. During the Try, the down box shall display the point value (1, 2, or 3) declared by A and be placed at the goal line.

Section 4. Required Player Equipment

Article 1. Jersey.

Players of opposing teams shall wear contrasting colored jerseys, without pockets, numbered on the front or rear. Players of the same team shall wear the same color or similar colored jerseys with different numbers. The visiting team is responsible for avoidance of similarity of colors. Jerseys shall be either

A. long enough so they remain tucked into the pants/shorts during the entire down or

B. **short enough so there is a minimum of 4" from the bottom of the jersey to the player's waistline. The Referee shall use a fist to measure the distance between the waistline and the bottom of the jersey.**

Article 2. Pants/Shorts.

Each player shall wear pants or shorts. **They shall be a different color than the flags.**

Article 3. Flag Belt.

Each player shall wear a one piece quick release belt, without any knots, at the waistline with 3 flags permanently attached, 1 flag on each side and 1 in the center of the back. The flags shall be a minimum of 2" wide and 14" long when measured from the edge of the belt. The flags should be of a contrasting color to the opponent's flags. The belt must have a spring loaded clip. NOTE: If the flags are not located on each hip and the tailbone, then the player must change to an appropriate size belt that meets the Rule.

PLAY. A-1 breaks the huddle not wearing a flag belt or the jersey is untucked as the 25 second count is running: (a) The Referee informs A-1 of the problem and as A-1 secures a flag belt or tucks in the jersey the 25 second count expires; or (b) the Referee points out the problem to A-1, who refuses to acquire a flag belt or tuck in the jersey; or (c) the Referee does not see A-1 without a flag belt as the ball is snapped and A-1 advances 25 yards before tagged by B-4; or (d) the Referee observes that A-1 or B-1 was not wearing a flag belt during the down. RULING. In (a), penalize A for delay of game. In (b), penalize A for unsportsmanlike conduct. In (c) and (d), the offended team can take the result of the play or penalize the offending team 5 yards from the previous spot for not wearing required equipment.

Article 4. Shoes.

Shoes shall be made of a canvas, leather, or synthetic material that covers the foot attached to a firm sole of leather, rubber, or composition material that may have cleats or be cleatless. Cleats are limited to studs or projections that do not exceed 1/2" in length and are made with nonabrasive rubber or rubber-type synthetic material that does not chip or develop a cutting edge. Rubber cleats with a tipped metal material are legal.

Article 5. Penalty.

Failure to wear required equipment in Articles 1-4. *Penalty:* Failure to Wear Required Player Equipment, 5 yards (S23). If it is a dead ball foul, 5 yards from the succeeding spot (S7 and S23).

Section 5. Optional Player Equipment

Article 1. Elastic Bandage.

Players may use an elastic bandage no more than 2 turns thick in any given area. It can be anchored at each end by tape not to exceed 2 turns.

Article 2. Gloves.

Players may wear gloves that must consist of a soft, pliable, and nonabrasive material.

Article 3. Headwear.
A. Players may wear a knit or stocking cap. The cap will have no bill. It can have a knit ball on top.
B. Players may wear a headband no wider than 2" and made of nonabrasive, unadorned, single-colored cloth, elastic, fiber, soft leather, or rubber. Rubber or cloth elastic bands may be used to control hair.
C. Players may wear a soft rubber hat.

Article 4. Pads.
Players may wear soft, pliable pads on the lower leg, knee, and ankle. Soft and yielding padded compression shorts and shirts are legal apparel.

Article 5. Mouth and Tooth Protector.
It is strongly recommended that a mouth piece be worn by all players.

Article 6. Play Books.
A. Players may carry a play book inside their clothing made of a yielding material only and must not be visible. If carried on the field, a player must keep the play book rather than throw it on the ground.
B. Players may wear a soft, pliable wrist/forearm band that contains plays.

Article 7. Sunglasses.
Players may wear pliable and non-rigid sunglasses.

Article 8. Face Shield.
Players may wear a face shield molded to the face with no protrusions to protect against a facial injury.

Section 6. Illegal Player Equipment
A player wearing illegal equipment shall not be permitted to play. This applies to any equipment that, in the opinion of the Referee, is dangerous or confusing. Types of equipment or substances that shall always be declared illegal include the following:

A. Headwear containing any hard, unyielding, stiff material, including billed hats, or items containing exposed knots. EXCEPTION: Face shield.
B. Jewelry.
C. Pads or braces worn above the waist. Casts worn above or below the waist.
D. Shoes with ceramic, screw-in, detachable cleats, or any projecting metal. EXCEPTION: Screw-in cleats are allowed if the screw is part of the cleat.
E. Shirts or jerseys that do not remain tucked in. Any hood on a coat, sweatshirt, or shirt that does not remain tucked in. Tear-away jerseys or jerseys that have been altered in any manner that produces a knot-like protrusion or creates a tear-away jersey. Jerseys that have an arm opening more than 4" below the armpit. The Referee will use a fist to measure the distance of the jersey arm opening.

F. Pants or shorts with any belt(s), belt loop(s), pocket(s), or exposed drawstring(s).

G. Leg and knee braces made of hard, unyielding material, unless covered on both sides and all edges overlapped, and any other hard substance unless covered with at least 1/2" of closed-cell, slow-recovery rubber, or other material of similar thickness and physical properties.

H. Any slippery or sticky foreign substance on any equipment or exposed part of the body.

I. Equipment that includes computers or any electronic or mechanical devices for communication.

J. Exposed metal on clothes or person. **This includes "O" or "D" rings used to secure flag belts.**

K. **Towels attached at the player's waist.**

L. **Flags that can be detached from the flag belt.**

M. **Hand warmers worn around the waist.**

Penalty: Unsportsmanlike Conduct, Illegal Player Equipment, 10 yards (S27).

PLAY. A-10 enters the field wearing illegal player equipment: (a) the Referee sees it prior to the snap or (b) the Referee sees it either during or after the down. **RULING.** In (a), the Referee will inform A-10 to return to the team box to repair or replace the illegal equipment. In (b), the Referee will enforce an unsportsmanlike conduct penalty against A-10.

Section 7. Missing or Illegal Player Equipment

When any required player equipment is missing or when illegal equipment is found on any incoming substitute or player, correction shall be made before participation. An official's time-out shall be declared to permit prompt repair of equipment that becomes illegal or defective through use.

Section 8. Coaches' Field Equipment

Local Area Network (LAN) phones and/or headsets may be used by coaches, other nonplayers, and players. However, players may use LAN phones and/or headsets only during authorized sideline conferences.

Penalty: Unsportsmanlike Conduct, 10 yards (S27).

RULE 2. DEFINITIONS OF PLAYING TERMS

Section 1. Ball Status; Dead, Live, and Loose

Article 1. Dead Ball.

A dead ball is a ball not in play. The ball is dead during the interval between downs.

Article 2. Live Ball.

A live ball is a ball in play. A ball becomes live when the ball is legally snapped and a down is in progress.

Article 3. Loose Ball.

A loose ball is a pass, fumble, or a kick. A loose ball that has not yet touched the ground is in flight. A grounded loose ball is one that has touched the ground. Any loose ball continues to be a loose ball until a player secures possession of it or until it becomes dead by Rule, whichever comes first.

Article 4. When the Ball Is Ready for Play.

A dead ball is ready for play when the Referee sounds the whistle and signals ready for play (S1).

Section 2. Batting

Batting is intentionally slapping, striking, or redirecting the ball with the hand or arm.

Section 3. Catch, Interception, Simultaneous Catch, and Touching

Article 1. Catch.

A catch is the act of establishing player possession of a live ball that is in flight by first contacting the ground inbounds while maintaining possession of the ball.

- A. If 1 foot first lands inbounds and the receiver has possession and control of the ball, it is a catch or interception even though a subsequent step or fall takes the receiver out of bounds.
- B. A catch by any kneeling or prone inbounds player is a completion or interception.
- C. It is not a catch or interception if a player's initial contact with the ground causes a loss of player possession and either the ball contacts the ground or the player is out of bounds prior to regaining player possession. NOTE: If in doubt, it is not a catch.

Article 2. Interception.

An interception is the catch of an opponent's fumble or pass.

Article 3. Recovery.

A recovery is gaining possession of a live ball after it strikes the ground.

Article 4. Simultaneous Catch or Recovery.

A simultaneous catch or recovery is a catch or recovery in which there is joint possession of a live ball by opposing players who are inbounds.

Article 5. Touching.

Catching is always preceded by touching the ball; thus, if touching causes the ball to become dead, securing possession of the ball has no significance. Touching refers to any contact with the ball.

Section 4. Down and Between Downs

A down is a unit of the game and starts, after the ball is ready for play, with a legal snap and ends when the ball next becomes dead. Between downs is the interval during which the ball is dead.

Section 5. Encroachment

Encroachment is a term to indicate a player is illegally in the neutral zone. An entering substitute is not considered to be a player for encroachment restrictions until they are on their side of the neutral zone.

Section 6. Field Areas

Article 1. The Field.

The field is the area within the sidelines and end lines, which includes both end zones.

Article 2. Field of Play.

The field of play is the area within the sidelines and goal lines.

Article 3. Side Zones.

The side zones are the areas bounded by the sidelines, hash marks, and goal lines.

Article 4. End Zones.

The end zones are located at each end of the field, between the goal line and the end line. The goal line is in the end zone, and a team's end zone is the one it is defending.

Article 5. Restricted Area.

The restricted area is the 2 yard belt between the sidelines and the team box, and it extends around the entire perimeter of the field. While coaches may occupy this area while the ball is dead, all nonplayers must vacate the restricted area when the ball is live.

Section 7. Fighting

Fighting is any attempt by a player or nonplayer to strike or engage an opponent in a combative manner unrelated to football. Such acts include, but are not limited to, attempts to strike an opponent(s) with the arm(s), hand(s), leg(s), or foot (feet), whether or not there is contact.

Section 8. Foul and Flagrant Foul

Article 1. Foul.

A foul is a rule infraction for which a penalty is prescribed. NOTE: If in doubt, it is not a foul.

Article 2. Flagrant Foul.

A flagrant foul is so severe or extreme that it places an opponent in danger of serious injury and/or involves violations that are extremely or persistently vulgar or abusive conduct.

Section 9. Fumble

A fumble is a loss of player possession other than by handing, passing, or punting the ball.

Section 10. Goal Line

Each goal line is a vertical plane separating the end zone from the field of play. The plane of the goal line extends beyond the sideline.

Section 11. Handing the Ball

Handing the ball is transferring player possession from 1 teammate to another without throwing or punting it.

Section 12. Huddle

A huddle is 2 or more offensive players grouped together after the ball is ready for play and before assuming scrimmage formation prior to the snap.

Section 13. Hurdling

Hurdling is an attempt by a player to jump (hurdle) with 1 or both feet or knees over an opponent who is contacting the ground with no part of their body except 1 or both feet.

Section 14. Kicks

Article 1. Kicker.

The kicker is any player who legally punts. The kicker is a runner until they actually punt the ball.

Article 2. Legal and Illegal Kicks.

A legal kick is a punt by a player of the team in possession when such a kick is permitted by Rule. Any punt continues to be a punt until it is caught by a player or becomes dead. Kicking the ball in any other manner is illegal.

Article 3. Punt.

A punt is made by K under restrictions that prohibit either team from advancing beyond their scrimmage lines until the ball is punted. A player becomes a kicker when their knee, lower leg, or foot makes contact with the ball before it strikes the ground.

Section 15. Loss of a Down

Loss of a down means loss of the right to repeat the down.

Section 16. Muff

A muff is an unsuccessful attempt to catch a ball, with the ball being touched in the attempt.

Section 17. Neutral Zone

The neutral zone is from the forward point of the football 1 yard to B's scrimmage line and extended to each sideline. It is established when the ball is marked ready for play.

Section 18. Passes

Article 1. Passer.
The passer is the player who has thrown a legal forward pass flight or until they move to participate in the play.

Article 2. Passing.
Passing the ball is throwing it. In a pass, the ball travels i caught, intercepted, or the ball becomes dead. The initial di or backward.

Article 3. Forward Pass and Backward Pass.
A forward pass is a pass thrown with its initial direction tov is a pass thrown with its initial direction parallel with or toward the passer's end line. A backward pa fumble that hits the ground is ruled dead at that spot.

Section 19. Penalty
A penalty is a result imposed by Rule against a team or team member that has committed a foul.

Section 20. Possession
A ball in player possession is a live ball held or controlled by a player after it has been handed or snapped to them, or after they caught or recovered it. A ball in team possession is a live ball that is in player possession or one that is loose following loss of such player possession. A live ball is always in the possession of a team. A change of possession occurs when the opponent gains player possession during the down.

Section 21. Removing the Flag Belt

Article 1. Flag Belt Removal.
🏈 When the flag belt is clearly taken from the runner in possession of the ball, the ball is declared dead and the down shall end. If a flag belt inadvertently falls to the ground, a 1 hand tag between the shoulders and knees constitutes capture. A player may leave their feet to remove the flag belt.

Article 2. Contact.
🏈 In an attempt to remove the flag belt from a runner, an opponent may contact the body, but not the face, neck, or any part of the head of the runner, with their hands. An opponent may not hold, push, or knock the runner down in an attempt to remove the flag belt.

Section 22. Screen Blocking
Screen blocking is legally obstructing an opponent without using any part of the body to initiate contact.

Section 23. Scrimmage Line
The scrimmage line for A is the yard line and its vertical plane that passes through the forward point of the ball. The scrimmage line for B is the yard line and its vertical plane that passes 1 yard from the point of the ball nearest its own goal line. B's scrimmage line may extend into their end zone.

Section 24. Shift

...or more offensive players who, after a huddle or after taking set positions, move ...before the ensuing snap.

Section 25. Spots

Basic Spot.

...sic spot is a point of reference for penalty enforcement. See 10-2.

Article 2. Enforcement Spot.

The enforcement spot is the point from which a penalty is enforced.

Article 3. Dead Ball Spot.

The dead ball spot is the spot under the foremost point of the ball when it becomes dead by rule. EXCEPTIONS: See 7-6-4B, 7-6-5B, and 8-8-1A EXCEPTION.

Article 4. Inbounds Spot.

The inbounds spot is the intersection of the hash marks and the yard line

- A. through the forward point of the ball when the ball becomes dead in a side zone; or
- B. through the forward point of the ball on the sideline between the goal lines when a loose ball goes out of bounds; or
- C. through the spot under the forward point of the ball in the possession of a runner when they cross the plane of the sideline and goes out of bounds.

Article 5. Out-of-Bounds Spot.

The out-of-bounds spot is where the ball becomes dead because of going out of bounds.

Article 6. Post Scrimmage Kick Spot.

The post scrimmage kick spot is the spot where the kick ends. R retains the ball after penalty enforcement from the post scrimmage kick spot when a post scrimmage kick foul occurs. The post scrimmage kick spot is the 14 yard line for kicks that result in a touchback. Fouls by R behind the post scrimmage kick spot are spot fouls.

Article 7. Previous Spot.

The previous spot is where the ball was last snapped.

Article 8. Spot of a Foul.

The spot of a foul is where the foul occurs. If a foul occurs out of bounds, the spot of the foul is at the intersection of the nearer hash mark and the yard line extended on which the foul occurs.

Article 9. Spot Where a Run Ends.

The spot where a run ends is:

- A. where the ball becomes dead if the runner does not lose possession or if the runner's fumble/backward pass from beyond the scrimmage line touches the ground or goes out of bounds behind the spot of the fumble/backward pass;

B. where the player loses possession if their run is followed by their fumble/backward pass that touches the ground or goes out of bounds beyond the spot of the fumble/backward pass, their illegal forward pass, or their fumble/backward pass beyond the scrimmage line is intercepted; or

C. the spot of the catch or recovery when the momentum rule is in effect.

Article 10. Succeeding Spot.

The succeeding spot is where the ball would next be snapped if a foul had not occurred. When a foul occurs during a down in which a touchdown is scored, as in 10-3-10, the succeeding spot may, at the option of the offended team, be the succeeding spot after the Try.

Section 26. Tagging

Tagging is placing 1 hand anywhere between the shoulders and knees, including the hand and arm, of an opponent with the ball. The tagger may leave their feet to make the tag. Pushing, striking, slapping, and holding are not permitted. If the player trips the runner in their attempt to make a diving tag, it is a foul.

Section 27. Player and Team Designations

Article 1. A and B.

A is the team that snaps the ball. The opponent of A is B. A player of A is A-1 and teammates are A-2 and A-3. Other abbreviations are B-1 for a player of B, K-1 for a player of the kickers, and R-1 for a receiver.

Article 2. Disqualified Player.

A disqualified player is one who becomes ineligible and is removed from further participation in the game.

Article 3. Offensive and Defensive Team.

The offensive team is the team in possession or the team to which the ball belongs. The defensive team is the opposing team.

Article 4. Player and Nonplayer.

A player is any one of the participants in the game. A nonplayer is a coach, trainer, other attendant, a substitute, or a replaced player who does not participate by touching the ball, hindering an opponent, or influencing the play.

Article 5. Runner.

The runner is the player in possession of a live ball or simulating possession of a live ball. Once a player catches or intercepts a pass, they become a runner.

Article 6. Snapper.

The snapper is the player who snaps the ball.

Article 7. Substitute.

A substitute is a team member who may replace a player.

RULE 3. PERIODS, TIME FACTORS, AND SUBSTITUTIONS

Section 1. Start of Each Half

Article 1. Coin Toss.

3 minutes before the start of the game the Referee shall instruct the visiting captain to give a "heads" or "tails" choice before the coin toss. The Referee will then toss the coin in the presence of the opposing captains. All officials shall be present for the coin toss.

The captain winning the toss shall have the 1st choice of options for the 1st half or shall defer (S10) their option to the 2nd half. The options for each half shall be as follows:

    A. To choose whether their team will start on offense or defense.

    B. To choose the goal their team will defend.

The captain who did not win the 1st choice of options for a half shall exercise the remaining option.

Article 2. Change Periods.

Between the 1st and 2nd and between the 3rd and 4th periods, the teams shall change goals. Team possession, number of the next down, and the zone line-to-gain remain unchanged.

Article 3. Forfeit Time.

Game time is forfeit time.

Article 4. Start 1st and 3rd Periods.

Unless moved by penalty or field dimensions have been shortened, the ball shall be snapped on the 14 yard line to start the 1st and 3rd periods.

Section 2. Game Time

Article 1. Playing Time and Intermissions.

Playing time shall be 48 minutes, divided into 4 periods of 12 minutes each. The intermission between the 2nd and 3rd periods shall be 5 minutes. When overtime is used, there will be a 3 minute intermission. NOTE: Timing rules may be modified due to institutional program needs.

Article 2. Interrupted and Shortened Games.

    A. When thunder is heard or a cloud-to-ground lightning bolt is seen, suspend play immediately. Wait at least 30 minutes prior to resuming play. If subsequent thunder is heard or lightning is seen after the beginning of the 30-minute count, reset the clock and another 30-minute count will begin. NOTE: If in doubt, consider the safety of all participants to be paramount to the game.

    B. When weather conditions are construed to be hazardous to life or limb of the participants, the crew of officials is authorized to delay or suspend the game.

    C. By mutual agreement of the opposing captains or head coaches and the Referee, any remaining period may be shortened or the game terminated at any time.

D. Games interrupted because of events beyond the control of the responsible administrative authority shall be continued from the point of interruption, unless the Referee and the opposing captains and/or head coaches agree to terminate the game with the existing score, or there are institutional or governing body rules that apply.

Article 3. Extension of Periods.

A period shall be extended by an untimed down (S1) if 1 of the following occurred during a down in which time expires:

A. There was a foul by either team and the penalty is accepted, except for: (1) unsportsmanlike or nonplayer fouls, (2) fouls that specify loss of down, (3) fouls on a scoring play that are enforced following the Try, or (4) fouls for which enforcement by rule result in a safety. NOTE: For loss of down fouls, any score by the team that fouls is cancelled.
B. There was a double foul.
C. There was an inadvertent whistle.
D. If a touchdown was scored, the Try is attempted unless the touchdown is scored during the last down of the 4th period and the point(s) would not affect the outcome of the game or playoff qualifying. NOTE: The Try shall always be attempted as part of the same period as the touchdown it follows.

If (A), (B), or (C) occurs during the untimed down (S1), the procedure is repeated. NOTE: The period shall not be extended further when the defense fouls during a successful Try and the offended team accepts the results of the play with enforcement of the penalty from the succeeding spot.

PLAY. As time expires in the 1st period, A-3 scores a touchdown and spikes the ball. B elects to enforce the penalty from B's 14-yard line to start their next series. **RULING:** Following the Try, the 1st period ends. The 2nd period shall begin following enforcement of A-3's unsportsmanlike conduct penalty.

Article 4. Game Timer.

It is recommended that playing time be kept on a stop watch operated by the Back Judge.

Article 5. First 22 Minutes of Each Half.

The clock shall start on the snap. It will run continuously for the first 22 minutes of each half unless it is stopped for one of the following reasons:

A. Team time-out – clock restarts on the snap. NOTE: If a team time-out is called prior to a Try, the Try down shall be untimed, and the clock shall restart on the snap of the play that follows the Try.
B. Official's time-out – clock restarts on the ready for play.
C. End of the 1st or 3rd period – clock restarts on the snap.

PLAY. With 10:20 remaining in the 2nd period, A-2 requests, and is granted, a timeout. The next down is (a) 3rd down or (b) a Try down. **RULING.** In (a), the clock will start on the snap. In (b), the clock will start on the snap of the play that follows the Try.

Article 6. 2 Minute Warning.

Approximately 2 minutes before the end of the 2nd and 4th periods, the Referee shall stop the clock and inform both captains of the playing time remaining in that period. The clock starts on the snap. The Back Judge will announce to the captains the remaining time and status of the clock after every play during the final 2 minutes of the 2nd and 4th periods.

Article 7. Last 2 Minutes.

During the final 2 minutes of the 2nd and 4th periods the clock will stop for one of the following reasons:

    A. Incomplete legal or incomplete illegal forward pass – clock restarts on the snap.

    B. Out of bounds – clock restarts on the snap.

    C. Safety – clock restarts on the snap.

    D. Team time-out – clock restarts on the snap.

    E. First down – clock restart is dependent on the previous play.

    F. Touchdown – clock restarts on the snap (after the Try).

    G. Penalty and administration – clock restart is dependent on the previous play (EXCEPTION: Delay of game foul is accepted – clock restarts on the snap).

    H. Official's time-out – clock restarts at their discretion.

    I. Touchback – clock restarts on the snap.

    J. A is awarded a new series – clock restart is dependent on the previous play.

    K. B is awarded a new series – clock restarts on the snap.

    L. Either team is awarded a new series following a legal punt – clock restarts on the snap.

    M. Team attempting to conserve time illegally (includes intentional grounding and a backward pass thrown intentionally out of bounds) – clock restarts on the ready.

    N. Team attempting to consume time illegally – clock restarts on the snap.

    O. Inadvertent whistle – clock restarts on the ready.

PLAY. Inside the final 2 minutes of the 2nd or 4th periods, A-1: (a) advances the ball across the zone line-to-gain and is deflagged inbounds; or (b) advances the ball across the zone line-to-gain, runs 5 more yards, and flag guards before stepping out of bounds. **RULING.** In (a), the clock stops for the 1st down and will restart when the Referee marks the ball ready for play. In (b), the clock stops for the player stepping out of bounds and will restart on the snap, regardless of whether the penalty is accepted.

Article 8. Correct Timing Errors.

The Referee shall have authority to correct obvious timing errors if discovery is prior to the 2nd live ball following the error unless the period has officially ended.

PLAY. A-23 is deflagged inbounds short of the line-to-gain on 1st down with 1:24 remaining in the 4th period. With the play clock at 5 seconds on the 2nd down, the back judge announces the game clock is at 1:24. **RULING.** The Referee may correct the obvious timing error, because it was recognized prior to the 2nd live ball following the error. The play clock shall be reset to 25 seconds, the game clock shall be reset to 1:04, and the Referee may use their discretion to start the game clock on either the ready for play or the snap.

Article 9. Ending a Period.
End the period following a short delay to ensure

    A. no foul has occurred,

    B. no obvious timing error has occurred,

    C. no request for a coach-Referee conference has occurred, or

    D. no other irregularity has occurred.

The Referee shall hold the ball in 1 hand overhead (S14) to indicate the period has officially ended.

Section 3. Tie Game

Article 1. Mandatory Meeting.
If a game ends with a tie score, the officials shall bring all players and coaches of both teams to the center of the field. They shall discuss the tie breaker procedures and answer all questions prior to the coin toss. After this meeting, the captains will stay while the remaining players and coaches return to their respective team box.

Article 2. Coin Toss.
A coin will be tossed by the Referee to determine the options as in the start of the game. The visiting captain shall call the toss. There will be only 1 coin flip during the overtime. If additional overtime periods are played, captains will alternate choices. The winner of the toss shall be given options of offense, defense, or direction. The loser of the toss shall make a choice of the remaining options. All overtime periods are played toward the same goal line.

Article 3. Tie Breaker.
Unless moved by penalty, each team shall start 1st and goal from B's 10 yard line. The object will be to score a touchdown. An overtime period consists of a series of 4 downs by each team. If the score is still tied after 1 period, play will proceed to a 2nd period or as many as are needed to determine a winner. If the 1st team awarded the ball scores, the opponent will still have a chance to win the game. A Try will be attempted and scored as indicated in Rule 8. When B secures possession, the ball is dead and the series is over. The ball will be placed at B's 10 yard line, and the original defense will begin their series of 4 downs, if available. Each team is entitled to only 1 time-out during the entire overtime.

Article 4. Fouls and Penalties.
Fouls and penalties are administered similar to the regular game. A shall be awarded a new series of 4 downs when an automatic 1st down foul is accepted. Dead ball fouls following a touchdown are penalized

on the Try. Dead ball fouls following a successful Try will be penalized from the succeeding spot, B's 10 yard line, if accepted. NOTE: The goal line shall *always* be zone line-to-gain in overtime, regardless of the number of overtimes played.

Section 4. Time-Outs

Article 1. How Charged.
The Referee shall declare a time-out when they suspend play for any reason. Each time-out shall be charged either to the Referee or 1 of the teams.

Article 2. Official's Time-Out.
The Referee shall declare an official's time-out when an excess time-out is allowed for an injured player. The Referee may declare an official's time-out for any contingency not covered elsewhere by the Rules. If a time-out is for repair or replacement of player equipment that becomes illegal through play and is considered dangerous to other players, the time-out is charged to the Referee.

Article 3. Charged Time-Outs.
Each team is entitled to 3 charged time-outs during each half. Successive charged time-outs may be granted to each team during a dead ball period. If the ball is dead and a team has not exhausted its charged time-outs, the Referee shall allow a time-out and charge that team or complete a coach-Referee conference. NOTE: Number of time-outs may be modified due to institutional program needs.

Article 4. Length of Time-Outs.
A charged time-out requested by any player, player-coach, or head coach that is legally granted shall be 1 minute and can be shortened if both teams are ready. Other time-outs may be longer only if the Referee deems it necessary.

Article 5. Coach-Referee Conference.
When a team requests a charged time-out for a misapplication or misinterpretation of a Rule, the Referee and 1 other official will confer with the captain, player-coach, or head coach. The request must be made prior to the time the ball becomes live following the play to be reviewed unless the half has officially ended. If the Referee changes their ruling, it is an official's time-out. If the ruling is not changed, it is a charged time-out. If the team has used its available time-outs, a delay of game penalty will be assessed.

Article 6. Notification.
The Referee shall notify both teams 5 seconds before a charged time-out expires. When 3 time-outs have been charged to a team in a half, the Referee shall notify both captains, both head coaches, and all officials. NOTE: The Referee will communicate the number of team time-outs remaining for each team to the A and B captains and all officials after each charged time-out is taken.

Article 7. Authorized Conferences.
There are 2 types of authorized conferences permitted during charged time-outs:

A. Players and nonplayers may meet directly in front of the team box within 5 yards of the sideline; or

B. One coach or player-coach may enter their team's huddle between the hash marks to confer with no more than 7 players **(Co-Rec Rule: 8 players)**.

Article 8. Injured Player.

An injured or apparently injured player who is discovered by an official while the ball is dead and the clock is stopped shall be replaced for at least 1 down unless the halftime or overtime intermission occurs. A player who is bleeding, has an open wound, or has any amount of blood on their uniform shall be considered an injured player.

PLAY. Near the end of the 1st period, K-2 falls to the ground and is slow to get up: (a) the nearest official declares an official's time-out for injury, or (b) K-2 gets up and leaves the field under their own power without an official's time-out being declared. In both cases, the Referee then signals the ready-for-play and time expires prior to the next snap. **RULING.** In (a), K-2 is an injured player and must remain off the field for at least one play. In (b), K-2 may participate for the first play of the 2nd period.

Article 9. Concussion.

Any player who exhibits signs, symptoms, or behaviors consistent with a concussion (such as loss of consciousness, headache, dizziness, confusion, or balance problems) shall be immediately removed from the game and shall not return to play until cleared by an appropriate health care professional.

Section 5. Delay of Game

The ball must be put in play promptly and legally. Any action or inaction by either team that tends to prevent this is delay of game. This includes any of the following:

A. Failure to snap within 25 seconds after the ball is declared ready for play.

B. Putting the ball in play before it is declared ready for play.

C. Deliberately advancing the ball after it is declared dead.

D. Coach-Referee Conference after all permissible charged time-outs for the coach's team have been used, and during which the Referee is requested to reconsider the application of a Rule and no change results.

Penalty: Dead Ball Foul, Delay of Game, 5 yards from the succeeding spot (S7 and S21).

Section 6. Illegally Conserving or Consuming Time

When a team attempts to conserve or consume time illegally, the Referee shall order the clock started or stopped. If the kicking team delays kicking the ball, as described in 6-1-4, the Referee may also reset the clock to the time of the previous snap and start the clock on the snap. When a penalty is accepted with less than 2 minutes remaining in either half, the offended team will have the option to start the game clock on the snap. *Penalty:* Illegally Consuming Time, 5 yards from the previous spot (S19). NOTE: If in doubt, apply a penalty for Illegally Consuming Time.

PLAY. As the game clock is running near the end of a period, A stalls and allows the 25 second count to expire. **RULING.** Delay of game penalty. The Referee shall order the game clock started on the next snap.

PLAY. A, losing, is deflagged with 10 seconds left in the game. They line up quickly and snap the ball prior to the Referee marking it ready for play. There are 2 seconds on the clock. **RULING.** Delay of game penalty. The Referee will start the game clock on the ready as A is attempting to conserve time. Prior to sounding the whistle, the Referee will inform the A captain or head coach that the game clock will start on the ready.

PLAY. During the 4th period, A leads B 14-12 with the game clock running. A-3 false starts with 50 seconds remaining on the game clock. **RULING.** Enforce false start, if accepted. The Referee will order the game clock started on the snap due to A attempting to consume time.

PLAY. Fourth and 15. K announces a punt. There are 2 minutes remaining in the 1st half when the ball is snapped. K-2 snaps the ball to K-3, who holds the ball for 6 or 7 seconds and then punts it out of bounds. Approximately 15 seconds run off the clock. **RULING.** The Referee will enforce Illegally Consuming Time. Penalize K 5 yards from the previous spot. Reset the game clock to 2 minutes and start the clock on the snap. **NOTE:** If the penalty is accepted, it may only be enforced at the previous spot.

Section 7. Substitutions

Article 1. Eligible Substitutions.

Between downs any number of eligible substitutes may replace players provided the substitution is completed by having the replaced players off the field before the ball is snapped. An incoming substitute must enter the field directly from their team area. A replaced player must leave the field immediately at the sideline nearest their team area prior to the ball being snapped. An entering substitute shall be on their team's side of the neutral zone when the ball is snapped. *Penalty:* Illegal Substitution, 5 yards (S22). If it is a dead ball or nonplayer foul, 5 yards from the succeeding spot (S7 and S22).

PLAY. A has 8 players on the field. A-8 realizes this and runs toward their end line to get off the field. They step over the end line: (a) prior to the snap; or (b) after the ball is snapped. **RULING.** Illegal substitution. In (a), dead ball foul and (b), live ball foul.

Article 2. Legal Substitutions.

During the same dead ball interval, no substitute shall become a player and then withdraw, and no player shall withdraw and then re-enter as a substitute unless a penalty is accepted, a dead ball foul occurs, there is a charged time-out, or a period ends. *Penalty:* Dead Ball Foul, Illegal Substitution, 5 yards from the succeeding spot (S7 and S22).

RULE 4. BALL IN PLAY, DEAD BALL, AND OUT OF BOUNDS

Section 1. Ball in Play: Dead Ball

Article 1. Dead Ball Becomes Live.

A dead ball, after having been declared ready for play, becomes a live ball when it is snapped legally.

Article 2. Ball Declared Dead.

A live ball becomes dead and an official shall sound their whistle or declare it dead when one of the following occurs:

A. The ball goes out of bounds.

B. Any part of the runner other than a hand(s) or foot (feet) touches the ground.

PLAY. QB A-1 rolls out and slips, but regains their balance as the ball in contact with their hand touches the ground. **RULING.** Play continues as a ball in possession is considered part of the hand.

C. A touchdown, touchback, safety, or successful Try is made.

D. The ball strikes the ground following 1st touching by K.

E. K catches a punt that is beyond the neutral zone or when an untouched punt comes to rest on the ground and no player attempts to secure it.

F. A forward pass strikes the ground or is caught simultaneously by opposing players.

G. A backward pass or fumble by a player strikes the ground or is caught simultaneously by opposing players. A snapped ball that hits the ground before or after getting to the intended receiver is dead at the spot where it hits the ground. NOTE: If in doubt, a snap close to the ground remains live.

H. A forward pass is legally completed or a loose ball is caught by a player on, above, or behind the opponent's goal line.

I. **A runner has a flag belt removed legally by an opponent. A flag belt is removed when the clip is detached from the belt, the belt is torn into more than 1 piece, or the flag is torn off the belt (flag only). NOTE: If in doubt, the flag belt has been pulled.**

J. **A runner is legally tagged (flag only).**

PLAY. As A-1 is running down the field with the ball, their flags fall off and their shirt comes untucked. B-1 tags A-1's loose shirt tail but does not make contact with the body of A-1. **RULING:** A-1 is down at the spot at which B-1 contacts their shirt.

K. A runner is legally tagged with 1 hand between the shoulders and knees, including the hand and arm (touch only).

PLAY. B-2 deflags/tags A-4 after the passed ball is touched by A-4 and: (a) the ball is muffed then caught by A-4; or (b) the ball is muffed then intercepted by B-2; or (c) the ball is muffed then touched by B-2 and finally caught by A-4. **RULING.** In (a), (b), and (c), the ball is live and reverts to a 1 hand tag in (a) and (c). The ball becomes dead when the runner is tagged/deflagged legally.

L. A passer is deflagged/tagged prior to releasing the ball. NOTE: If in doubt, the ball is released.

M. A muff of a punt strikes the ground.

N. K's punt breaks the plane of R's goal line.

O. B secures possession during a Try or overtime.

P. A prosthetic device becomes dislodged from a player who is in possession of the ball.

Q. An official sounds their whistle inadvertently during a down or during a down in which the penalty for a foul is declined and the status of the ball is as follows:

1. The ball is in player possession. The team in possession may elect to put the ball in play where declared dead or replay the down.

2. The ball is loose from a fumble, backward pass, illegal kick, or illegal forward pass. The team in possession may elect to put the ball in play where possession was lost or replay the down.

3. The ball is in flight during a legal forward pass or a punt. The ball is returned to the previous spot and the down replayed.

If a foul occurs during any of the above downs, an accepted penalty shall be administered as in any other play situation. When the foul is accepted, disregard the inadvertent whistle. NOTE: There is no time added to the game clock during a down with an inadvertent whistle.

Section 2. Succeeding Spot

Article 1. Placement of Dead Ball.
When the ball becomes dead between the hash marks, play is resumed at the dead ball spot. If the ball becomes dead in a side zone, place the ball at the nearest hash mark at the corresponding yard line.

Article 2. Anywhere Between the Hash Marks.
Before the ready for play signal, A may designate the spot from which the ball is put in play anywhere between the hash marks for the start of each half; for a Try; following a touchback, safety, Try, and awarded catch after a punt; for the start of each series in overtime.

Section 3. Out of Bounds

Article 1. Player Out of Bounds.
A player or other person is out of bounds when any part of the person is touching anything, other than another player or official, that is on or outside the sideline or end line.

PLAY. A-8 leaps to catch a pass at the goal line near the sideline. After controlling the ball in the air, A-8's foot contacts the pylon. A-8 then lands in the end zone. **RULING.** Incomplete pass.

Article 2. Player in Possession Out of Bounds.

A ball in player possession is out of bounds when the runner or the ball touches anything, other than another player or official, that is on or outside the sideline or end line.

Article 3. Loose Ball Out of Bounds.

A loose ball is out of bounds when it touches anything, including a player or official, that is out of bounds.

RULE 5. SERIES OF DOWNS, NUMBER OF DOWNS, AND TEAM POSSESSION AFTER PENALTY

Section 1. A Series: How Started, How Broken, How Renewed

Article 1. A Down Is a Unit.

A down is a unit of the game that starts with a legal snap and ends when the ball next becomes dead. Between downs is any period when the ball is dead.

Article 2. Series of Downs.

A shall have 4 consecutive downs to advance to the next zone. Any down may be repeated or lost if provided by the Rules.

Article 3. Zone Line-to-Gain.

The zone line-to-gain in any series shall be the zone in advance of the ball, unless distance has been lost due to penalty or failure to gain. In such case, the original zone in advance of the ball at the beginning of the series of downs is the zone line-to-gain. The forward point of the ball, when declared dead between the goal lines, shall be the determining factor.

Article 4. Awarding a New Series.

A new series of downs shall be awarded when a team moves the ball into the next zone on a play free from penalty; or a penalty against the opponents moves the ball into the next zone; or an accepted penalty against the opponents involves an automatic 1st down; or after enforcement of a penalty against A, the ball is in advance of the zone line-to-gain; or either team has obtained legal possession of the ball as a result of a penalty, punt, touchback, pass interception, or failure to gain the zone in advance of the ball.

NOTE: If in doubt, the out-of-bounds punt is "short" of the zone line-to-gain.

Article 5. Incorrect Down.

Until a new series is awarded, the Referee shall have authority to correct an error in the number of downs.

Section 2. Down and Possession After a Penalty

Article 1. Penalty Resulting in a 1st Down.

After a penalty that leaves the ball in the possession of a team beyond its zone line-to-gain, or when a penalty stipulates a 1st down, the down and distance established by that penalty shall be 1st down with next zone line-to-gain.

PLAY. Third and 10 from A's 10. A-2 flag guards at A's 25 and runs to B's 30, where they are deflagged. **RULING.** After enforcement of the penalty, it will be 3rd and 5 from A's 15.

PLAY. Fourth and 5 from A's 15. A-1 throws an illegal forward pass beyond A's scrimmage line: (a) at A's 23 and the ball hits the ground. (b) at A's 26 and the ball hits the ground. **RULING.** In (a), B's ball on A's 18,

1st down and goal to go. Since the 5 yard penalty put A 2 yards short of the zone line-to-gain on 4th down, the loss of down awards the ball to B. In (b), A is penalized 5 yards and loss of down, which puts the ball on A's 21, 1st down and 19. Even though an illegal forward pass carries a loss of down, since the 5 yard penalty enforcement places the ball beyond the 20 yard line, it is 1st down for A.

Article 2. Foul Before Change of Team Possession.

Following a distance penalty between the goal lines that occurs during a down and before any change of team possession during that down, the ball belongs to A. The down shall be repeated unless the penalty also involves loss of a down, or leaves the ball on or beyond the zone line-to-gain. If the penalty involves loss of a down, the down shall count as 1 of the 4 in that series.

Article 3. Foul After Change of Team Possession.

Following a distance penalty for a foul committed after team possession has changed during that down, the ball belongs to the team in possession when the foul occurred. The down and distance established by that penalty shall be 1st down with zone line-to-gain.

PLAY. B-4 intercepts a pass by A-1 and returns it to A's 25. During the run by B-4, B-2 makes illegal contact with A-6 at A's 29. **RULING.** B is penalized 10 yards utilizing the All-But-One Enforcement Principle (10-2-2) from A's 29—the spot of the foul. It is B's ball, 1st down and 19. B obtained the ball with "clean hands."

Article 4. Penalty Declined.

If a penalty is declined, the number of the next down shall be whatever it would have been if that foul had not occurred.

Article 5. Rule Decisions Final.

A Rules decision may not be changed after the ball is next legally snapped.

RULE 6. KICKING THE BALL

Section 1. Punt

Article 1. Legal Punt.

A legal punt is a kick made in accordance with the Rules. Quick punts are illegal. *Penalty:* Illegal Kick, Quick Punt, 10 yards (S31).

Article 2. Punt.

Prior to marking the ball ready for play on 4th down, the Referee must ask the A captain if they want to punt. The Referee must announce this decision to all A and B players and all officials (S43). The A captain may declare a punt on any down. After such announcement, the ball must be punted. EXCEPTION: If (a) an A or B time-out is called, (b) the period ends, (c) a foul occurs, or (d) an inadvertent whistle is blown anytime prior to or during this down after the A captain's decision that results in the kicking team having the right to repeat the down again, the Referee must ask the A captain whether or not they want to punt and communicate this decision to the B captain (S43).

PLAY. Fourth and 22. The Referee asks the A captain if they want to punt or "go for it." The A captain delays their decision. **RULING.** The Referee can enforce Illegally Consuming Time and stop the game clock, if they think the A captain is using delaying tactics.

Article 3. Crossing the Scrimmage Line.

Neither K nor R may enter the neutral zone until the ball is punted. *Penalty:* Illegal Procedure, 5 yards (S19). NOTE: Rules 7-1, 7-2, and 7-3 apply prior to and during the snap only.

Article 4. Punting the Ball.

After receiving the snap, the kicker must punt the ball immediately in a continuous motion. *Penalty:* Illegal Procedure, 5 yards (S19). NOTE: See 3-6.

Article 5. After Being Punted.

Once the ball is punted, any R player may block the kick. If the blocked punt hits the ground, it is dead at that spot. If the punt is blocked by any R player behind K's scrimmage line and then caught by any K player behind K's scrimmage line (1st ball spotter–orange), K may run and/or throw a pass. R may advance the punt anywhere in the field of play. A K player cannot punt the ball to any K player, including the kicker. K may punt the ball only once per down. *Penalty:* Illegal Kicking, 10 yards (S31).

PLAY. Fourth and 5 at K's 35. K-1's punt is blocked by R-1, who contacts the ball at K's 36. The ball is then caught by K-1 at K's 30. K1 (a) is immediately deflagged, (b) throws an incomplete forward pass, or (c) runs to R's 30, where they are deflagged. **RULING.** First down for K from (a) K's 30, (b) K's 35, and (c) R's 30. R's touching of the kick beyond R's scrimmage line broke the continuity of downs, so a new series shall be awarded to the team in possession at the end of the down.

Article 6. Punt Crosses K's Scrimmage Line.

When a punt that has crossed K's scrimmage line (1st ball spotter–orange), touches a player from either team and then hits the ground, the ball is dead and belongs to R. If it hits an R player and then is caught in the air, it can be advanced by R. If the ball hits an R player beyond R's scrimmage line and is then caught by K beyond R's scrimmage line, the ball is dead, belongs to K, and a new series begins for K.

PLAY. R-1, attempting to catch a punt, muffs the ball. K-3 catches the ball before it hits the ground and runs for a touchdown. **RULING.** K's ball at the spot where the ball was caught, 1st down and zone line-to-gain. During a punt, K cannot advance a muff by R. However, K can advance an airborne fumble by R because the punt has ended with possession.

Article 7. 1st Touching.

If any K player touches a punt after it crosses K's scrimmage line (1st ball spotter–orange) and before it is touched there by any R player, it is referred to as "1st touching" (S16). R may take the ball at that spot or may choose to have the ball put in play as determined by the action that follows 1st touching. The right of R to take the ball at the spot of 1st touching by K is cancelled if R touches the punt and thereafter during the down commits a foul or if the penalty is accepted for any foul committed during the down.

PLAY. K-1's punt bounces at R's 15. K-2 attempts to recover the kick to down the ball but muffs it at R's 19. The ball strikes the ground at R's 22. **RULING.** K-2 is guilty of first touching. R may choose to have the ball at either R's 19 (the spot of first touching) or R's 22 (the dead ball spot).

Article 8. Punt Out of Bounds Between the Goal Lines or at Rest.

If a punt goes out of bounds between the goal lines or comes to rest untouched in the field of play and no player attempts to secure it, the ball becomes dead and belongs to the receiving team at that spot.

Article 9. Punt Behind the Goal Line.

When a punt breaks the plane of R's goal line, it is a touchback unless R chooses the spot of 1st touching by K.

Section 2. Kick Catching Interference

While any punt is in flight beyond K's scrimmage line (1st ball spotter–orange), K shall not touch the ball or R, nor obstruct R's path to the ball, unless the punt has been touched by R. K may catch, touch, muff, or bat a punt in flight beyond K's scrimmage line if no R player is in position to catch the ball. *Penalty:* Kick Catching Interference, 10 yards (S33).

PLAY. R-1, attempting to catch a punt, touches the ball and the ball is then caught by K-1 before striking the ground. **RULING.** Not interference. Protection against kick catching interference ceases when any R player touches the ball. It is dead where caught and belongs to K, 1st down and zone line-to-gain.

PLAY. A punt is in flight and: (a) K-3 is in the path of R-2's attempt to catch the ball, or (b) K-4 tags or deflags R-2 before they touch the ball. **RULING.** In (a) and (b), Kick Catching Interference.

PLAY. A punt is in flight and K-1 touches the ball: (a) R-1 is in position to catch the kick, or (b) no receiver is in position to catch the kick. **RULING.** (a) Kick Catching Interference. (b) There is no Kick Catching Interference since no receiver was in a position to catch the kick.

Section 3. Signals
Players shall ignore any signals given by K or R. The ball remains live.

RULE 7. SNAPPING, HANDING, AND PASSING THE BALL

Section 1. The Scrimmage

Article 1. The Start.

All plays must be started by a legal snap next to the orange ball spotter, which is on or between the hash marks. The ball may be moved with approval by the Referee due to poor field conditions.

Article 2. Ball Responsibility.

A players are responsible for retrieving the ball after a down. The snapper will bring the ball from the huddle to the A scrimmage line (1st ball spotter–orange). A small towel may be placed under the ball, regardless of weather or field conditions.

Article 3. Stances.

Players may use a 2, 3, or 4 point stance.

Section 2. Prior to the Snap

Article 1. Encroachment.

Following the ready for play signal and until the snap, no B player may encroach or touch the ball, nor may any player contact opponents or interfere with them in any other way. This includes standing in the neutral zone to give defensive signals or shifting through the zone. After the snapper has placed their hand(s) on the ball, it is encroachment for any player to break the scrimmage line plane, except for the snapper's right to be over the ball. *Penalty:* Dead Ball Foul, Encroachment, 5 yards from the succeeding spot (S7 and S18). During the interval between downs when 2 or more encroachment fouls are committed by B, the penalty will be 10 yards for the subsequent encroachment fouls.

PLAY. After the ball is marked ready for play by the Referee, B-4 charges into the neutral zone beyond B's scrimmage line (2nd ball spotter–gold), to give A a 1st down. **RULING.** Dead Ball Foul, Encroachment, 5 yards. The penalty is declined by A. B is informed by the Referee that if this foul occurs again during the same dead ball interval, a 10 yard penalty will be enforced, if accepted.

Article 2. False Start.

No A player shall make a false start. A false start includes simulating a charge or start of a play. An infraction of this Rule may be penalized whether or not the ball is snapped and the penalty for any resultant encroachment shall be cancelled. *Penalty:* Dead Ball Foul, False Start, 5 yards from the succeeding spot (S7 and S19).

Article 3. Snap.

The snapper, after assuming position for the snap at A's scrimmage line (1st ball spotter–orange) and adjusting the ball, may neither move nor change the position of the ball in a manner simulating the beginning of a play until it is snapped. An infraction of this provision may be penalized, whether or not the ball is snapped, and the penalty for any resultant encroachment foul by an opponent shall be cancelled. When over the ball, the snapper shall have their feet behind their scrimmage line (1st ball spotter–orange). The snapper shall pass the ball back from its position on the ground/towel/orange ball spotter with a quick and continuous motion of the hand(s). The ball shall leave the hand(s) in this motion. There is no Rule restriction regarding placement of the long axis of the ball at right angles to A's scrimmage line. NOTE: The snapper may have one or both knees on the ground during the snap. *Penalty:* Dead Ball Foul, Illegal Snap, 5 yards from the succeeding spot (S7 and S19).

Article 4. Disconcerting Act.
No defensive player shall use disconcerting acts or words prior to the snap in an attempt to interfere with A's signals. *Penalty:* Dead Ball Foul, Disconcerting Act, 5 yards from the succeeding spot (S7 and S23).

PLAY. B-1 calls defensive signals loudly: (a) before A gets set; or (b) while A is yelling cadence or audibles. B-1 is not using words similar to A's cadence or audibles. **RULING.** Legal in (a) and (b).

Section 3. Position and Action During the Snap

Article 1. Legal Position.
Anytime on or after the ball is marked ready for play, each A player must momentarily be at least 5 yards inbounds before the snap. NOTE: If a B player covers an A player positioned within 5 yards of the sideline, it is not a foul. *Penalty:* Illegal Formation, 5 yards (S19).

Article 2. Minimum Line Players.
The snapper is the only A player required to be on their scrimmage line (1st ball spotter–orange) at the snap.

Article 3. Motion.
Only 1 A player may be in motion, but not in motion toward the opponent's goal line at the snap. Other A players must be stationary in their positions without movement of their feet, body, head, or arms. *Penalty:* Illegal Motion, 5 yards (S20).

PLAY. After a huddle, all A players come to a stop and remain stationary for a full second, then A-2 goes in motion legally and the ball is snapped. **RULING.** Legal.

Article 4. Direct Snap.
The player who receives the snap must be at least 2 yards behind A's scrimmage line (1st ball spotter–orange). The distance is determined by the point at which the ball is first touched following the snap. The snapper may not snap the ball to themself. *Penalty:* Illegal Formation, 5 yards (S19). NOTE: If in doubt, the A player 1st touched the snap 2 yards behind A's scrimmage line.

PLAY. A-1 is under the center. The center snaps the ball through the legs of A-1 to A-6, who is 5 yards behind A's scrimmage line and legally in motion. **RULING.** Legal. The snap was received by an A player who first touched the ball at least 2 yards behind A's scrimmage line.

Article 5. Shift.
In a snap preceded by a huddle or shift, all A players must come to a complete stop and remain stationary in legal position without movement of feet, body, head, or arms for at least 1 full second before the snap. *Penalty:* Illegal Shift, 5 yards (S20).

PLAY. A-1 goes in motion legally as A-2 moves to a new position in the backfield, sets, and the ball is snapped. **RULING.** Illegal Shift, 5 yards.

Section 4. Handing the Ball

Any player may hand the ball forward or backward at any time.

Section 5. Running the Ball – Co-Rec Rule

An A runner who is a man cannot advance the ball through A's scrimmage line (1st ball spotter-orange). There are no restrictions:

    A. Once the ball has been touched by any player beyond the A or K scrimmage line.

    B. During a run by a runner who is a woman.

    C. After a change of team possession.

    D. After a legal forward pass.

Penalty: **Illegal Advancement, 5 yards from the previous spot (S19).**

NOTE: See 7-7-3: Illegal Reception – Co-Rec Rule.

PLAY. A-1 (man) runs beyond A's scrimmage line and then: (a) retreats behind A's scrimmage line and throws a forward pass or (b) throws a backward pass to A-2 (woman), who throws a forward pass from behind A's scrimmage line. RULING. Illegal Advancement in both (a) and (b).

Section 6. Backward Pass and Fumble

Article 1. When Legal.

A runner may pass the ball backward or lose player possession by a fumble anytime except if intentionally thrown out of bounds to conserve time. *Penalty:* Illegal Pass, 5 yards from the spot of the pass or fumble and loss of down (S35 and S9). The Referee will start the clock on the ready for play. NOTE: If in doubt, the pass is backward. See 9-5.

Article 2. Caught or Intercepted.

A backward pass or fumble in flight may be caught or intercepted by any other player inbounds and advanced. A player may not throw an untouched backward pass to themselves. *Penalty:* Illegal Pass, 5 yards from the spot of the pass and loss of down if by A before possession changes during a scrimmage down (S35 and S9).

Article 3. Simultaneous Catch by Opposing Players.

If a backward pass or fumble in flight is caught simultaneously by members of opposing teams inbounds, the ball becomes dead at the spot of the catch and belongs to the offensive team.

Article 4. Out of Bounds.

A backward pass or fumble that goes out of bounds is dead. If the backward pass/fumble goes out of bounds between the goal lines, the ball belongs to the offensive team:

    A. at the out-of-bounds spot if it is behind the spot of the pass or fumble, or

    B. at the spot of the pass or fumble if it goes out of bounds beyond the spot of the pass or fumble.

If out of bounds behind a goal line, it is a touchback or safety.

Article 5. Ball Dead When It Hits the Ground.
A backward pass or fumble that touches the ground is dead. If the backward pass/fumble touches the ground in the field of play, the ball belongs to the offensive team:

    A. at the spot where it touches the ground if it is behind the spot of the pass or fumble, or

    B. at the spot of the pass or fumble if it touches the ground beyond the spot of the pass or fumble.

If the fumble/backward pass touches the ground in either end zone, it is a touchback or safety.

PLAY. Fourth and 2 at A's 38. A-1 takes the snap and, from A's 35, throws a backward pass to A-2, who muffs the ball. The ball lands at: (a) A's 30 or (b) B's 39. **RULING.** In (a), it shall be B's ball, 1st and 10 at A's 30. In (b), it shall be B's ball, 1st and 15 from A's 35.

PLAY. While standing in the field of play, A-1's fumble lands in: (a) A's end zone or (b) B's end zone. **RULING.** In (a), it is a safety: 2 points for B, and B will next snap the ball, 1st and 10 from B's 30. In (b), it is a touchback, and B will next snap the ball, 1st and 6 from B's 14.

PLAY. A-1 is standing in A's end zone when A-1 fumbles. The fumble goes out of bounds at A's 2. **RULING.** The ball is returned to the spot of the fumble. Safety: 2 points for B.

Section 7. Legal and Illegal Forward Pass
Article 1. Legal Forward Pass.
All players are eligible to touch or catch a pass. During a scrimmage down and before team possession has changed, a forward pass may be thrown provided the passer's feet are on or behind the plane of A's scrimmage line (1st ball spotter–orange) when the ball leaves the passer's hand. Only 1 forward pass can be thrown per down. NOTE: If in doubt, the passer is behind the A scrimmage line.

PLAY. A-1 runs with the ball beyond the A scrimmage line, then returns behind the A scrimmage line and throws a forward pass. **RULING.** Legal play.

PLAY. A-1 throws a backward pass from A's 31 yard line that is caught by A-6 at A's 33 yard line. **RULING.** Legal play. The initial direction of a pass determines whether the pass is forward or backward. While a backward pass may have its flight path altered by wind or forward player momentum and subsequently be caught beyond the point of release, this does not change the status of the pass.

PLAY. A-1 throws a legal forward pass that is controlled by airborne A-2. Prior to returning to the ground, A-2 throws the ball forward or backward to A-3, who runs for a touchdown. **RULING.** Legal play. The pass remains a pass until A-2 alights on the ground for a completion. Since A-2 is airborne, they may bat or throw the legal forward pass in any direction.

Article 2. Illegal Forward Pass.

A forward pass is illegal

- A. if the passer's foot is beyond the plane of A's scrimmage line (1st ball spotter–orange) when the ball leaves their hand.
- B. if a passer catches their untouched forward pass.
- C. if there is more than 1 forward pass per down.
- D. if thrown after a team possession has changed.
- E. if intentionally thrown to the ground or out of bounds to save loss of yardage or conserve time.

Penalty: (A, B, & C) Illegal Forward Pass, 5 yards from the spot of the pass and a loss of down (S35 and S9). (D) Illegal Forward Pass, 5 yards from the spot of the pass (S35). (E) Intentional Grounding, 5 yards from the spot of the pass and a loss of down (S36 and S9).

PLAY. A-1 throws a short forward pass: (a) A-1 catches; (b) the ball is tipped by A-4, or B-3, then A-1 catches; or (c) A-6 catches pass and throws a backward pass to A-1. **RULING.** In (a), illegal forward pass. In (b) and (c), the play is legal as another player touched the ball before A-1 again possessed it. However, A cannot throw a 2nd forward pass during the down.

PLAY. QB A-1 catches the snap from the center and IMMEDIATELY throws the ball into the ground to stop the clock. **RULING.** This play is legal provided the QB is not trying to avoid a loss of yardage.

Article 3. Illegal Reception – Co-Rec Rule.

- **A. The term "open" (S40) means any player can complete a legal forward pass to any other player. The term "closed" (S41) means a player who is a man may NOT complete a legal forward pass to any other player who is a man. NOTE: All illegal forward pass fouls are classified as fouls during a running play. Thus, illegal forward passes do not change the open/closed status of a down.**
- **B. The 1st down of each half or overtime possession shall be open. The 1st down of a new series following a team change of possession shall be open.**
- **C. If the crew of officials erroneously indicate the open/closed status of a down, the play is nullified and the down will be repeated.**
- **D. During the offensive team's possession there may not be 2 consecutive legal forward pass completions from a player who is a man to a receiver who is a man. This Rule applies to the Try.**
- **E. If a passer who is a man completes a legal forward pass to a receiver who is a man, the next legal forward pass completion must involve either a passer who is a woman or receiver who is a woman for positive yards. The spot where the ball becomes dead by Rule must be beyond A's scrimmage line (1st ball spotter–orange). There is NO foul for a receiver who is a woman being tagged or deflagged behind A's scrimmage line. The next legal forward pass completion remains closed.**

F. A legal forward pass caught jointly by teammates who are a man and a woman is considered a reception by a woman.

G. There are no other restrictions concerning a passer who is a man completing legal forward passes to a receiver who is a woman, or a woman to a woman, or a woman to a man.

H. If a receiver who is a man catches a pass from a passer who is a man on a closed play, it is a foul for Illegal Reception. Whether the penalty is accepted or declined, the next down shall remain closed.

I. Any other foul, whether accepted or declined, shall have no effect on whether the next legal forward pass completion is open or closed.

Penalty: Illegal Reception, 5 yards from the previous spot, and a loss of down (S19 and S9). The next down is closed.

PLAY. Second and 15 on A's 25. The down is closed—the last legal forward pass completion was man to man. (a) A-1 (man) throws a legal forward pass caught by A-2 (woman) at A's 23. A-2 runs to A's 26 and is deflagged; or (b) same play, except A-2 is deflagged at A's 24. RULING. (a) The next down is open. A gained positive yards. In (b) there is no foul. The next down is still closed. A did not gain positive yards. The dead ball spot was behind the A scrimmage line.

PLAY. Second and 7 on A's 13. This down is closed. A-1 (man) completes a legal forward pass to A-2 (woman) at A's 19. After the catch, A-2 guards her flag belt at A's 22. RULING. If accepted, enforce guarding the flag belt, 10 yards from the spot of the foul. It would be A's ball 2nd and 8 on A's 12. All fouls carry their usual enforcement. The next down will be open since there was a man to woman legal forward pass completion, and the ball became dead beyond the A scrimmage line. Whether the foul is accepted or declined has no effect on open or closed restrictions.

PLAY. The down is closed. A-1 (man) completes a pass to A-2 (woman) for positive yards. A-3 commits illegal contact and B-2 roughs the passer. RULING. Double foul. Repeat the down. The down is open since A-2 caught a pass for positive yards.

PLAY. Second and 14 at A's 6. Closed play. QB A-1 (man) is 5 yards deep in A's end zone when he throws a forward pass that is caught by A-2 (man): (a) 2 yards deep in A's end zone, (b) at A's 3, or (c) at A's 10. In all cases, A-2 is deflagged at A's 21. RULING. Illegal Reception in (a), (b), and (c). Acceptance of the penalty results in 3rd and 17 at A's 3. The play will be closed.

Article 4. After Illegal Forward Pass.
When an illegal forward pass touches the ground or goes out of bounds, the ball becomes dead and belongs to the passing team at the spot from where the pass was thrown, unless a new series of downs has been created. In such a case the ball belongs to the passing team if, after enforcement of the penalty, the ball is left in advance of the zone line-to-gain, or belongs to the opponents if the ball, after the penalty, did not make the next zone line-to-gain and the foul occurred during 4th down. If a player catches an illegal forward pass, the ball continues in play until declared dead.

Section 8. Completed or Intercepted Passes

Article 1. Pass Caught or Intercepted.

A forward pass is completed when caught by a member of the passing team inbounds. A forward pass is intercepted when caught by a member of the opposing team inbounds. It is counted as a completion or interception as long as the 1st part of the receiver to make contact with the ground after the catch, usually 1 foot, touches inbounds.

PLAY. A-1 throws a forward pass that is low and near the ground to A-2, who appears to make the catch. **RULING.** The officials must visibly see the ball strike the ground to rule incomplete. If an official does not see the ball hit the ground, it will be ruled a completed pass.

PLAY. A-1 throws a forward pass to A-2. Prior to catching the forward pass, A-2 steps out of bounds on the sideline, possesses the ball in flight, and lands inbounds. **RULING.** Completed pass (it might be Illegal Participation, see 9-6-1G).

Article 2. Simultaneous Catch by Opposing Players.

If a forward pass is caught simultaneously by members of opposing teams inbounds, the ball becomes dead at the spot of the catch and belongs to the offensive team.

Section 9. Incomplete Pass

When a forward pass touches the ground or anything out of bounds, it becomes dead.

Section 10. Forward Pass Interference

Article 1. Interference.

During a down in which a legal forward pass crosses A's scrimmage line (1st ball spotter–orange), contact that interferes with an eligible receiver who is beyond A's scrimmage line (1st ball spotter–orange) is pass interference unless it occurs when 2 or more eligible receivers make a simultaneous and bona fide attempt to reach, catch, or bat a pass. It is also pass interference if an eligible receiver is deflagged/tagged prior to touching a forward pass thrown beyond A's scrimmage line (1st ball spotter–orange).

PLAY. A-1 throws a legal forward pass toward A-5, who is beyond A's scrimmage line. Before A-5 touches the pass, B-2 deflags A-5. **RULING.** Defensive pass interference.

PLAY. B-1 defending against a legal forward pass beyond A's scrimmage line, waves their arms in the face of A-2, who is attempting to catch the pass but does not make contact with A-2. **RULING.** Legal play.

Article 2. Offensive Pass Interference.

After the ball is snapped and until the pass has been touched by any player there shall be no offensive pass interference beyond A's scrimmage line (1st ball spotter–orange). *Penalty:* Offensive Pass Interference, 10 yards from the previous spot (S33).

Article 3. Defensive Pass Interference.

After the pass is thrown and until the pass has been touched by any player there shall be no defensive pass interference beyond A's scrimmage line (1st ball spotter–orange) while the pass is in flight. *Penalty:* Defensive Pass Interference, 10 yards from the previous spot (S33). If the pass interference by either player is intentional or unsportsmanlike, their team shall be penalized an additional 10 yards (S27).

PLAY. A-3 muffs a legal forward pass and B-2 pushes A-3 out of the way in an attempt to secure the ball. **RULING.** Personal foul for illegal contact, penalize 10 yards.

Article 4. Not Interference.

Contact by B that is obviously away from the direction of the forward pass is not pass interference but may be a personal foul.

Article 5. Catchable/Uncatchable.

Whether a pass is catchable or uncatchable has no bearing on offensive and defensive forward pass interference.

RULE 8. SCORING PLAYS AND TOUCHBACK

Section 1. Communication

The Referee will communicate the current score to the A and B captains, head coaches, and all officials after each touchdown, Try, and safety. If there is a disagreement regarding the current or final score, the Referee will make the final decision after consulting with the other officials and, if available, the scorekeeper.

Section 2. Forfeited Game

The score of a forfeited game shall be: Offended Team-1, Opponent-0. If the offended team is ahead at the time of the forfeit, the score stands. A Referee's decision to forfeit a game is final.

Section 3. Mercy Rule

Article 1. 2 Minute Warning.

If a team is 19 or more points ahead when the Referee announces the 2 minute warning for the 4th period, the game shall be over. Prior to implementing the Mercy Rule, the Referee shall apply the Extension of Period Rule (3-2-3). NOTE: Game clock starts according to Rule 3.

PLAY. Score: A-10, B-36. With 2:10 remaining in the 4th period, QB A-1 throws a pass to A-2. B-1 commits defensive pass interference. Pass falls incomplete. Game clock is at 2:00. **RULING.** Penalty is enforced and play continues. Mercy Rule is not applied until a down free of any accepted live ball fouls occurs. The clock starts on the snap.

PLAY. Score: A-10, B-36. A scores a touchdown with 2:10 remaining on the clock in the 4th period. **RULING.** A must call a team time-out to stop the clock prior to the 2 minute warning in order to go for a 2 point Try. If A trails by 19 or more points when the Referee announces the 2 minute warning, the Mercy Rule is enforced and the game is over.

Article 2. After 2 Minute Warning.

If a team scores during the last 2 minutes of the 4th period and that score creates a point differential of 19 or more points, the game shall end at that point.

Section 4. Player Responsibility

The player scoring must raise their arms so the nearest official can deflag the player. If the player is not able to be deflagged and the official determines the flag belt has been secured illegally, the score is disallowed, the offending team is penalized, and the player is disqualified. *Penalty:* Personal Foul, Tampering with the Flag Belt, 10 yards from the previous spot (S38 and S47). If by A, loss of down (S9). If by B, automatic 1st down (S8).

Section 5. Touchdown Value: 6 Points

It is a touchdown when a runner advances from the field of play so that the ball penetrates the vertical plane of the opponent's goal line. It is a touchdown when a loose ball is caught by a player while the ball is on or behind the opponent's goal line.

Section 6. Try Value: 1, 2, or 3 Points

Article 1. Referee's Responsibility and Team's Choice.

The Referee must speak to the coach or captain, asking them whether the Try shall be from the 3, 10, or 20 yard line. Once the A coach/captain makes the choice, they may change the decision only when an A or B charged time-out is taken. The value of the Try may not be changed if a dead ball foul occurs after the ready for play signal, or if a live ball foul occurs during the Try. The Referee will ask the scoring coach/captain where they would like the ball placed on or between the hash marks. Enforcement of yardage penalties does not change the value of the Try. The point(s) shall be awarded if the Try results in what would have been a touchdown.

Article 2. 1, 2, or 3 Points.

An opportunity to score 1 point from the 3 yard line, 2 points from the 10 yard line, or 3 points from the 20 yard line by running or passing only shall be granted the team scoring a touchdown. NOTE: If a touchdown is scored on the last timed down of the 4th period, the Try is not attempted, unless it will affect the outcome of the game or playoff qualifying.

Article 3. Try Begins and Ends.

The Try begins when the ball is marked ready for play. The Try ends when B secures possession, the Try is successful, or the ball becomes dead by Rule. B cannot score during the Try.

Article 4. Next Play.

After a Try, the ball shall be snapped by the opponent of the scoring team at their own 14 yard line, unless moved by penalty or to begin overtime.

Section 7. Force and Responsibility

Article 1. Force.

The force imparted by a player who punts, passes, snaps, or fumbles the ball shall be considered responsible for the ball's progress in any direction even though its course is deflected, or reversed, after striking the ground or after striking a player of either team. However, the initial force is considered expended and a new force is provided if a loose ball is illegally kicked or batted or it is contacted again after coming to rest.

PLAY. Second and 16 on A's 4. A-1 throws a backward pass that is batted by B-1 at the A 2. The ball lands in A's end zone. **RULING.** Safety. The force that put the ball in A's end zone was the backward pass.

Article 2. Responsibility.

The team responsible for a ball being on, above, or behind a goal line is the team whose player

A. carries the ball to or across that goal line.
B. imparts to the ball an impetus that forces it to or across that goal line.
C. incurs a penalty that leaves the ball on or behind the goal line.

Section 8. Momentum, Safety, and Touchback

Article 1. Safety Value: 2 Points.

It is a safety when one of the following occurs:

A. A runner carries the ball from the field of play to or across their own goal line, and it becomes dead there in their team's possession. This includes when a player's fumble or backward pass from inside their own end zone lands or goes out of bounds between the goal lines.

EXCEPTION: Momentum Rule: When a defensive player intercepts their opponent's forward pass, fumble, or backward pass, or an R player catches or recovers a punt between their 5 yard line and the goal line and their original momentum carries them into the end zone where the ball is declared dead in their team's possession behind the goal line, the ball belongs to the defensive team at the spot where possession was gained.

PLAY. B-1 intercepts A-1's pass or fumble at: (a) B's 4 or (b) B's 6. In both cases, the player's momentum takes them into B's end zone, where they take a knee. **RULING.** In (a), the momentum rule is in effect. It shall be B's ball, 1st and 16 at B's 4. In (b), it is a safety: 2 points for A.

PLAY. R-1 catches or recovers K-1's punt at (a) R's 4 or (b) R's 6. In both cases, the player's momentum takes them into R's end zone, where they take a knee. **RULING.** In (a), the momentum rule is in effect. It shall be R's ball, 1st and 16 at R's 4. In (b), it is a safety: 2 points for K.

B. A player punts, passes, fumbles, snaps, muffs, or bats a loose ball from the field of play to or across their goal line and the ball subsequently becomes dead there in their team's possession. This includes when the ball is declared dead on or behind their goal line. However, it does not apply to a legal forward pass that becomes incomplete.

PLAY. A-1, after receiving the snap in their end zone, is deflagged/tagged with the ball above the goal line, its forward point in the field of play. **RULING.** Safety. The entire ball has to be in the field of play when taking it out of your own end zone.

C. A player on offense commits any foul for which the penalty is accepted and measurement is from a spot in their end zone; or throws an illegal forward pass from their end zone and the penalty is declined in a situation that leaves them in possession at the spot of the illegal pass and with the ball having been forced into the end zone by the passing team.

D. After a safety, the ball shall be snapped by the scoring team at their own 30 yard line, unless moved by penalty.

Article 2. Touchback.

It is a touchback when 1 of the following occurs:

A. K's punt breaks the plane of R's goal line.

B. The ball is out of bounds behind a goal line (except from an incomplete forward pass), when the ball becomes dead in the possession of a player on, above, or behind the player's own goal line, or when the ball becomes dead not in possession on, above, or behind the team's own goal line and the attacking team is responsible. NOTES: If in doubt, it is a touchback. If in doubt, the out-of-bounds punt near the goal line is a touchback.

PLAY. B-1 intercepts a pass in their end zone: (a) runs for a touchdown; or (b) runs around in their end zone and is deflagged or steps across the end line. **RULING.** In (a), Touchdown. A player can run the ball out of their end zone. In (b), Touchback. A's force put the ball into B's end zone.

PLAY. A-1 running for an apparent touchdown fumbles the ball on B's 3 yard line. The ball lands in B's end zone. **RULING.** Touchback. The force that put the ball in the end zone was the fumble.

PLAY. K-4 punts to R-3, who touches the ball in flight at R's 4 yard line. The ball bounces off their hands and lands in R's end zone. **RULING.** Touchback. The initial force was imparted by K and the ball was never in the possession of R-3.

C. After a touchback, the ball shall be snapped from the nearest 14 yard line, unless moved by penalty.

RULE 9. CONDUCT OF PLAYERS AND OTHERS

Section 1. Unsportsmanlike Conduct

Article 1. Noncontact Acts.

No player or nonplayer shall commit noncontact acts during a period or intermission. Examples include, but are not limited to, the following:

A. Refusal to comply with or abide by the request or decision of an official
B. Intentionally kicking at the ball, other than during a punt
C. Leaving the field between downs to gain an advantage unless replaced or with permission of the Referee
D. Participate while wearing illegal player equipment
E. Being outside the team box, but not on the field, during a live ball. NOTE: During a dead ball, coaches can be a maximum of 2 steps on the field for coaching purposes only.

Penalty: Unsportsmanlike Conduct, 10 yards (S27) (S7 and S27 if dead ball). If flagrant in (A), (B), and (C), the offender shall be disqualified (S47). In (E) the 1st offense is a warning (S15), the 2nd offense is 5 yards (S7 and S29), and each subsequent offense is 10 yards (S7, S29, and S27).

Article 2. Dead Ball Fouls.

When the ball becomes dead in the possession of a player, they shall not

A. intentionally kick the ball,
B. spike the ball into the ground, or
C. throw the ball high into the air.

Penalty: Unsportsmanlike Conduct, 10 yards (S7 and S27), and if flagrant, the offender will be disqualified (S47).

Article 3. Prohibited Acts.

There shall be no unsportsmanlike conduct by players or nonplayers. Examples include, but are not limited to, the following:

A. Attempting to influence a decision by an official
B. Disrespectfully addressing an official
C. Indicating objections to an official's decision
D. Holding an unauthorized conference, or being on the field illegally
E. Using profanity or taunting, insulting, or vulgar language or gestures
F. Intentionally contacting a game official (DQ)
G. Leaving the team box and entering the field during a fight (DQ)

Penalty: Unsportsmanlike Conduct, 10 yards (S27) (S7 and S27 if dead ball), and if flagrant, the offender shall be disqualified (S47). In (F) and (G), the offender will be disqualified.

PLAY. Nonplayers voice disapproval using abusive language concerning a judgment call by the Back Judge. **RULING.** The Referee should call an "official's time-out." Inform the A captain and/or head coaches that such behavior is unacceptable and tell the captain to communicate this information to their bench. If such behavior is exhibited again during the game, penalize 10 yards for unsportsmanlike conduct. *It is imperative* that the officials stop such behavior the 1st time it occurs. A and B are present to play the game, not to officiate. When the officials accept the game assignment, they must be ready to take control.

Article 4. 2nd Unsportsmanlike Foul.
The 2nd unsportsmanlike foul by the same player or nonplayer results in disqualification.

Article 5. Ejection.
If a player or nonplayer is ejected from a game due to unsportsmanlike conduct, they may be allowed to remain on the bench. If the ejected player or nonplayer creates a problem for the game officials from the bench area, they will be told to leave the field area. The field area is defined as "out of sight, out of sound." If the ejected player or nonplayer refuses to leave after a reasonable amount of time, the Referee will inform the captain/coach that the game will be forfeited.

Article 6. 4th Unsportsmanlike Foul.
The 4th unsportsmanlike foul by the same team results in their forfeiture of the game. NOTE: By institutional adoption this number can be reduced to 3.

Section 2. Unfair Acts
Article 1. Refusal to Play or Halving the Distance.
If a team refuses to play within 2 minutes after being ordered by the Referee, or if a team repeatedly commits fouls that can be penalized only by halving the distance to its goal line, the Referee may enforce any penalty they consider equitable, including the awarding of a score. For refusal to play or for repeated fouls, the Referee shall, after 1 warning, forfeit the game to the opponents.

Article 2. Unfair Acts.
No player or nonplayer shall use verbiage or commit any act not in accordance with the spirit of fair play for the purposes of confusing the opponent. *Penalty:* Unfair Act, 10 yards (S38).

PLAY. (a) A-2 shouts to the Referee "wet ball, wet ball" in an attempt to have B relax. A-2 then snaps the ball and play begins; or (b) A-2 snaps the ball, but only 1 person leaves the scrimmage line. All other teammates stand up and yell at the person that the snap count was on 2. When B relaxes, A-1 throws the ball to the person who left the scrimmage line. **RULING.** In (a) and (b), Unfair Act. Use of verbiage or acts to gain an unfair advantage. Penalize using the All-But-One Enforcement Principle (10-2-2). Play (a) is a dead ball foul while (b) is a live ball foul. NOTE: Voice inflection by the QB is not an unfair act.

Section 3. Personal Fouls

Article 1. Restrictions.

No player or nonplayer shall commit a personal foul during a period or an intermission. Any other act of unnecessary roughness is a personal foul. Any player or nonplayer commits a personal foul when they take any of the following actions:

A. Strips or attempts to strip the ball from a runner by punching, striking, or grabbing the ball (S38). NOTE: Any player who controls a pass with both feet off the ground becomes a runner when the 1st part of the player touches the ground.

B. Throws the runner to the ground (S38)

C. Hurdles an opponent (S38)

D. Contacts an opponent either before or after the ball is declared dead (S38)

E. Makes contact of any nature with an opponent that is deemed unnecessary including using fists, locked hands, elbows, or any part of the forearm or hand, except according to the Rules (S38)

F. Drives or runs into an opponent (S38)

G. Positions their body on the shoulders or body of a teammate or opponent to gain an advantage (S38)

H. Tackles the runner by grasping or encircling with the hand(s) or arm(s) and taking the opponent toward the ground as in tackle football (S38 and S47) (DQ)

I. Fights an opponent (S38 and S47) (DQ). NOTE: Each player who participates in the fight will be assessed 1 flagrant personal foul for fighting.

J. Be in the restricted area and cause unintentional contact with a game official (nonplayers only).

Penalty: Personal Foul, 10 yards, and if flagrant, the offender will be disqualified (S47). In (H) and (I), the offender will be disqualified.

PLAY. B-2, moving toward A-1, who has the ball in their possession: (a) B-2 grabs/strips the ball from A-1; or (b) B-2 tries to knock the ball out of A-1's hands. **RULING.** In (a) and (b), this is a personal foul for stripping the ball. B-2 must go for the flag belt or the tag.

PLAY. A-1, running for a score, dives into the end zone: (a) breaks the plane with the ball without contacting any B player; (b) charges into B-3 at B's 1; or (c) charges into B-4 in the end zone after crossing the goal line. **RULING.** In (a), the score counts. In (b), a 10 yard penalty is assessed against A from B's 1. In (c), the score counts and A will be assessed a 10 yard dead ball penalty on the Try or at the 14.

PLAY. A-2 possesses A-1's pass in the air at B's 20. Prior to returning to the ground: (a) B-1 swats the ball out of A-2's hands without making other contact against A-2, or (b) B-1 makes illegal contact against A-2. In both cases, the ball comes out of A-2's hands and falls incomplete. **RULING.** No foul in (a) but illegal contact in (b). In (b), the penalty is enforced from the previous spot. **NOTE:** A player becomes a runner once they catch a pass by first contacting the ground inbounds while maintaining possession of the ball.

Article 2. Roughing the Passer.

Defensive players must make a definite effort to avoid charging into a passer after it is clear the ball has been thrown forward legally. No defensive player shall contact the passer who is standing still or fading back as they are considered out of the play after the pass. Roughing the passer restrictions do not apply if the forward pass is thrown from beyond A's scrimmage line (1st ball spotter–orange). *Penalty:* Roughing the Passer, 10 yards, automatic 1st down (S34 and S8).

PLAY. B-3 jumps to block a legal forward pass thrown by A-1 behind the scrimmage line and: (a) blocks the ball and, avoiding unnecessary contact, brushes A-1; (b) is unsuccessful in blocking the pass and charges into A-1; (c) blocks the ball and charges into A-1; or (d) contacts passer A-1's hand or arm. **RULING.** In (a), no foul; in (b), (c), and (d), roughing the passer, 10 yards and an automatic 1st down. If the rusher contacts the passer's hand or arm, whether or not they touch the pass, it is roughing the passer.

PLAY. B-3 contacts the arm of A-1, who is attempting to pass. Then the ball is: (a) fumbled, (b) not released, or (c) thrown backward. **RULING.** Personal Foul, Illegal Contact, 10 yards, in (a), (b), and (c). NOTE: Roughness by an opponent beyond the scrimmage line could be illegal contact against a player who throws an illegal pass beyond the scrimmage line.

Article 3. Screen Blocking.

An offensive screen block may occur anywhere on the field and shall take place without contact. The screen blocker shall have their hands and arms at their sides or behind their back when screen blocking. Any use of the hands, arms, elbows, legs, or body to initiate contact that displaces an opponent during a screen block is illegal. A blocker may use their hand(s) or arm(s) to break a fall or retain their balance. *Penalty:* Personal Foul, Illegal Contact, 10 yards (S38).

Article 4. Screen Blocking Fundamentals.

A player who screens shall not do any of the following:

    A. Initiate contact when blocking a stationary opponent from any direction.

    B. Prevent an opponent from avoiding contact by (1) taking a position closer than a normal step when behind a stationary opponent or (2) taking a position within 1 or 2 steps of a moving opponent so that the opponent cannot stop or change direction before contact.

    C. After taking a legal position, move to maintain it, unless the screener moves in the same direction and path as the opponent. If a screener violates any of these provisions and contact results, they have committed a foul.

Penalty: Personal Foul, Illegal Contact, 10 yards (S38).

Article 5. Interlocked Blocking.

Teammates of a runner or passer may legally screen block, but they shall not use interlocked blocking such as grasping or encircling one another in any manner. *Penalty:* Personal Foul, Interlocked Blocking, 10 yards (S38 and S44).

Article 6. Use of Hands or Arms by the Defense.

Opponents must go around the offensive player's screen block. The arms and hands may not be used as a wedge to displace the opponent. A defender may use their arms or hands to break a fall or retain their balance. *Penalty:* Personal Foul, Illegal Contact, 10 yards (S38).

Section 4. Runner

Article 1. Flag Belt Removal.

A. **Players must have possession of the ball before they can be deflagged legally by an opponent.**

B. **When a runner loses their flag belt either accidently, inadvertently (not removed by grabbing or pulling), or on purpose, play continues. The deflagging reverts to a 1 hand tag of the runner between the shoulders and knees by an opponent.**

C. **In circumstances where a flag belt is removed illegally by a player, play should continue with the option of a penalty on the play. *Penalty:* Personal Foul, Illegal Flag Belt Removal, 10 yards (S38).**

D. **An opponent intentionally pulling a flag belt from an offensive player without the ball is illegal. *Penalty:* Personal Foul, Illegal Flag Belt Removal, 10 yards (S38).**

E. **Tampering with the flag belt in any way to gain an advantage, including tying, using foreign materials, or other such acts, is illegal. *Penalty:* Personal Foul, Tampering with the Flag Belt, 10 yards from the previous spot, and player disqualification (S38 and S47). If by A, loss of down (S9). If by B, automatic 1st down (S8).**

F. **A nonplayer deflags or interferes with a runner. *Penalty:* Personal Foul, Nonplayer Deflagging/Interfering with the Runner, 10 yards (S38). The Referee will award a touchdown (S5) and disqualify (S47) the nonplayer.**

PLAY. A-1 carries the ball when B-1 and B-2 attempt to deflag the runner. B-1 and B-2 touch or grasp the flag belt momentarily. A-1 continues to run a few steps and the flag belt falls to the ground. RULING. A-1 is down where the original deflag was attempted. B-1 and B-2 are deemed to have caused the deflag.

Article 2. Guarding the Flag Belt.

A runner shall not flag guard by using their hands, arms, or the ball to cause contact between the runner and an opponent that denies the opponent the opportunity to pull or remove the flag belt. Examples of flag guarding include, but are not limited to, the following:

A. **Placing or swinging the hand or arm over the flag belt**

B. **Placing the ball in possession over the flag belt**

C. **Lowering the shoulders in such a manner that places the arm over the flag belt**

Penalty: **Flag Guarding, 10 yards (S24).**

PLAY. While the ball is covering A-1's flag belt, B-1 reaches out to grab A-1's flag. B-1 (a) did or (b) did not contact A-1. RULING. A-1 is guilty of flag guarding in (a). No foul occurred in (b).

Article 3. Stiff Arm.

The runner shall be prohibited from contacting an opponent with extended hand or arm. This includes the use of a "stiff arm" extended to ward off an opponent attempting to deflag/tag. *Penalty:* Personal Foul, Illegal Contact, 10 yards (S38).

Article 4. Help the Runner.

The runner shall not grasp a teammate or be grasped, pulled, or pushed by a teammate. *Penalty:* Help the Runner, 5 yards (S44).

Article 5. Obstruct the Runner.

An opponent shall not hold, grasp, or obstruct the forward progress of a runner when in the act of removing the flag belt or making a legal tag. *Penalty:* Holding, 10 yards (S42).

Article 6. Charge.

A runner shall not charge into nor contact an opponent in their path nor attempt to run between 2 opponents or between an opponent and a sideline, unless the space is such as to provide a reasonable chance for them to go through without contact. If a runner in their progress has established a straight line path, they may not be crowded out of that path, but if an opponent is able to legally establish a defensive position in that path, the runner must avoid contact by changing direction. *Penalty:* Personal Foul, Illegal Contact, 10 yards (S38).

PLAY. A-1 running toward B-2, who is attempting to deflag A-1: (a) goes around B-2 to avoid being deflagged; (b) deliberately runs through B-2 making no attempt to avoid contact; or (c) ducks their head while contacting B-2. RULING. In (a), Legal play. In (b) and (c), an A personal foul, 10 yards. If B-2 is stationary, A-1 must go around. The charge/block principles used in basketball apply.

Section 5. Batting and Kicking

Article 1. Batting a Loose Ball.

Players shall not bat a loose ball other than a pass or fumble in flight. EXCEPTION 1: A backward pass in flight shall not be batted or thrown forward by the passing team. EXCEPTION 2: K may bat a grounded or an airborne punt beyond K's scrimmage line toward their own goal line. *Penalty:* Illegal Batting, 10 yards (S31).

Article 2. Batting a Ball in Player Possession.

A ball in player possession shall not be batted forward by a player of the team in possession. *Penalty:* Illegal Batting, 10 yards (S31).

Article 3. Illegal Kicking.

No player shall intentionally kick a ball other than a punt. NOTE: An illegal kick shall be treated like a fumble. *Penalty:* Illegal Kicking, 10 yards (S31).

Section 6. Illegal Participation

The following actions are considered illegal participation:

A. To have 8 **(Co-Rec Rule: 9)** or more players participating at the snap.

B. **To have more than the legal number of men or women participating at the snap (Co-Rec Rule).**

C. If an injured player is not replaced for at least 1 down; unless the halftime or overtime intermission occurs.

D. To use a player, replaced player, or substitute in a substitution or pretended substitution to deceive opponents at or immediately before the snap.

E. For a disqualified player to reenter the game.

F. For a replaced player or substitute to hinder an opponent, touch the ball, influence the play, or otherwise participate.

G. If, prior to a change of possession, an A or K player goes out of bounds and returns inbounds during the down to participate, unless blocked out of bounds by an opponent. If a player is blocked out of bounds by an opponent and returns inbounds during the down, they shall return at the first opportunity. During the down, no player shall intentionally go out of bounds and return to the field, intentionally touch the ball, influence the play, or otherwise participate.

H. When any player, replaced player, or substitute enters during a down.

Penalty: Illegal Participation, 10 yards (S28).

PLAY. QB A-1 throws a legal forward pass to A-2. A-2 steps on the sideline, returns inbounds, and catches the pass. **RULING.** Completed pass, Illegal Participation, 10 yards.

RULE 10. ENFORCEMENT OF PENALTIES

Section 1. Procedure After a Foul

Article 1. Definitions.

A foul is a rule infraction for which a penalty is prescribed. Types of fouls are listed below:

  A. Dead Ball: A foul that occurs in the time interval after a down has ended and before the ball is next legally snapped.
  B. Live Ball: A foul that occurs during a down.
  C. Simultaneous With the Snap: An act that becomes a foul when the ball is snapped.

Article 2. Coach's/Captain's Choice.

When a foul occurs during a live ball, the Referee shall, at the end of the down, notify both coaches/captains. They shall inform the coach/captain of the offended team regarding the rights of penalty acceptance or declination and shall indicate to them the number of the ensuing down, distance to be gained, and status of the ball for each available choice. The distance penalty for any foul may be declined. If the penalty is declined or if there is a double foul, there is no loss of distance. The coach's/captain's choice of options may not be revoked. Decisions involving penalties shall be made before any charged time-out is granted.

PLAY. Third and 2 at A's 38. A-1's pass is incomplete, but B-2 is flagged for roughing the passer. **RULING.** First and 12 at B's 32 unless A elects to accept the penalty but decline the yardage. In that case, it is 1st and 2 at A's 38.

PLAY. B intercepts a pass at B's 3. After the interception, B-7 flag guards at B's 22 and is deflagged at B's 35. **RULING.** If A accepts the penalty, it is B's ball, 1st and 8 at B's 12. If A declines penalty, it is B's ball, 1st and 5 at B's 35. If A accepts the penalty but declines the yardage, it is B's ball, 1st and 18 at B's 22.

Article 3. Dead Ball Foul.

When a foul occurs during a dead ball either between downs or before a snap, the officials shall not permit the ball to become live. The penalty for any foul between downs, any nonplayer foul, or any unsportsmanlike foul, is enforced from the succeeding spot (EXCEPTION: 10-3-10 and 10-3-11). If a dead ball foul occurs after time expires for any period, the penalty shall be measured from the succeeding spot. The succeeding spot is where the ball would next be snapped if a foul had not occurred.

Article 4. Live Ball/Dead Ball Foul.

When a live ball foul by 1 team is followed by a dead ball foul by the opponent, the penalties are administered separately and in the order of occurrence. When the same team commits a live ball foul followed by 1 or more dead ball fouls, all fouls may be penalized.

Article 5. Establishing the Zone Line-to-Gain.

  A. On a live ball foul, mark off the penalty yardage first then establish the zone line-to-gain.

B. Penalties for fouls with succeeding spot enforcement that occur prior to the ready for play signal shall be administered before setting the zone line-to-gain down box for a new series.

C. Penalties for fouls with succeeding spot enforcement that occur after the ready for play signal shall be administered after setting the zone line-to-gain down box for a new series. NOTE: During overtime, the zone line-to-gain is always the goal line.

PLAY. Third and 2 on A's 18. A-2 runs to A's 26. (a) A-2 flag guards at A's 25 and is deflagged at A's 35; or (b) A-2 is deflagged at A's 26. The Referee calls an unsportsmanlike conduct foul on A-2 prior to the ready for play signal. **RULING.** (a) Penalize A 10 yards for flag guarding, A's ball 3rd and 5 on A's 15. (b) Penalize A 10 yards for the dead ball foul from A's 26, 1st and 4 on A's 16.

PLAY. On a 3rd down play, A achieves a 1st down at B's 38. Prior to the Referee blowing the ready for play whistle, A-2 snaps the ball and is flagged for delay of game. **RULING.** If accepted, it shall be 1st and 3 at A's 37.

PLAY. First and 18 at A's 22. (a) Prior to the ready for play whistle, A-3 snaps the ball and is flagged for delay of game, or (b) immediately following the ready for play whistle, A-2 is flagged for a false start. **RULING.** If accepted, in (a), it shall be 1st and 3 at A's 17, and in (b), it shall be 1st and 23 at A's 17.

Section 2. Types of Play and Basic Enforcement Spots
Article 1. Live Ball Fouls.

Any live ball foul is penalized according to the All-But-One Enforcement Principle (10-2-2), except as follows:

A. A foul that occurs simultaneously with the snap is penalized from the previous spot.

B. A nonplayer foul, unsportsmanlike foul, or dead ball foul is penalized from the succeeding spot.

C. A foul by K during a punting down (other than Kick Catching Interference or Illegally Consuming Time) may be penalized from the succeeding spot, at R's option, when K will not be next to put the ball in play.

PLAY. Fourth and 5 at K's 35. (a) K is flagged for illegal shift, or (b) K1 is flagged for crossing K's scrimmage line prior to the kick. R3 returns the kick to R's 25. **RULING.** In both (a) and (b), R may choose to enforce the penalty at either the previous spot (K's ball, 4th and 10 at K's 30) or the succeeding spot (R's ball, 1st and 10 at R's 30). R may also decline the penalty.

PLAY. Fourth and 5 at K's 35. (a) K is flagged for illegal shift, or (b) K-1 is flagged for crossing K's scrimmage line prior to the kick. R-3 muffs the kick, and K-3 catches it before it hits the ground at R's 20. **RULING.** In both (a) and (b), R may only enforce the penalty at the previous spot. It will be K's ball, 4th and 10 at K's 30.

Article 2. All-But-One Enforcement Principle.

Enforcement philosophy is based on the premise that a team is given the advantage of the distance that is gained without assistance of a foul. It is assumed that the only foul that would give this aid is a foul by the offense behind the basic spot. *Therefore, all fouls but this one, which is a foul by the offense behind the basic spot, are penalized from the basic spot.* This 1 foul is penalized from the spot of the foul (See Figure 1). EXCEPTION: Roughing the passer—see Article 4 below.

Article 3. 2 Types of Plays.

Whenever the ball is live, 1 of 2 types of plays is in progress, either a loose ball play or a running play. The type of play has no significance unless a foul occurs. If a foul does occur, the officials must know whether it was during a loose ball play or during a running play. This determines the basic spot of enforcement.

Article 4. Loose Ball Play.

A loose ball play is action during 1 of the following:

A. A punt, other than post scrimmage kick fouls

B. A legal forward pass

C. A backward pass (including the snap), illegal kick, or fumble made by A from on or behind their scrimmage line (1st ball spotter–orange) and prior to a change of team possession

D. The run or runs which precedes such legal pass, punt, or fumble

If a foul occurs during a loose ball play, the basic enforcement spot is the previous spot (2-25-7) (See Figure 3).

PLAY. First and 13 on A's 27. QB A-1 throws a legal forward pass. While the pass is in flight, A-2 illegally contacts a B player on A's 25. The pass is complete and the runner is deflagged on A's 30. **RULING.** If accepted, penalize from A's 25, 1st and 25 on A's 15. The penalty is enforced at the spot of the foul since the offense fouled behind the basic spot, which is the previous spot or where the ball was snapped.

EXCEPTION 1: The penalty for roughing the passer on a completed forward pass will be enforced from the dead ball spot when the run ends beyond A's scrimmage line and no change of possession has occurred.

PLAY. Fourth and 8 on A's 32. Passer A-1 is roughed by B-1: (a) forward pass is complete to A-2, who is tagged/deflagged at A's 35; (b) pass is incomplete; or (c) forward pass is complete to A-2, who is tagged/deflagged at A's 28. **RULING.** Roughing the passer. (a) A's ball, 1st and 15 on B's 35; in (b) and (c), it is A's ball, 1st and 18 on B's 38. In (b) and (c), penalize from the previous spot.

EXCEPTION 2: A post scrimmage kick (PSK) foul is an R foul that occurs on R's side of the neutral zone prior to the end of the kick during a punt that ends beyond the neutral zone and K does not have possession of the ball when the kick ends. The PSK spot is the spot where the kick ends. R retains the ball after penalty enforcement from the PSK spot when a PSK foul occurs. R fouls behind the PSK spot are spot fouls. The spot where the kick ends is R's 14 if the kick ends in R's end zone.

PLAY. During a punt, R-2 illegally contacts K-2 beyond the neutral zone at R's 34. The kick then becomes dead: (a) when the punt breaks the plane of R's goal line; (b) when the punt rolls out of bounds at R's 31; or (c) when R-1 catches the punt at R's 32 and is deflagged at R's 36. **RULING.** Enforce all 3 plays utilizing PSK penalty enforcement as follows: (a) Enforce at the PSK spot, R's 14, 1st and 13 at R's 7; (b) enforce at R's 31 since the spot of the foul is behind the PSK spot, 1st and 19 at R's 21; (c) enforce at the PSK spot, R's 32 where the punt was caught by R-1, 1st and 18 on R's 22. In (a), (b), and (c), R retains the football, 1st down.

EXCEPTION 3: Kick catching interference, 10 yards from the spot of the foul and a 1st down, or 10 yards from the previous spot and replay the down.

PLAY. Fourth and 10 at K's 30. During K-1's punt, K-2 is flagged for Kick catching Interference against R-1 at R's 25. R-1 returns the punt to R's 30, where they are deflagged. **RULING.** R has three options: decline the penalty, resulting in 1st and 10 at R's 30; accept a 10 yard penalty from the spot of the foul, resulting in 1st and 5 at R's 35; or accept a 10 yard penalty from the previous spot and a replay of the down, resulting in K's ball 4th and 20 at K's 20.

Article 5. Running Play.
A running play is any action that is not a loose ball play. There are 2 types of running plays:

   A. Behind the line, it includes
      1. a run that is not followed by a loose ball behind the line or
      2. a run that is followed by an illegal pass from behind the line.
   B. Beyond the line, it includes any run.

If a foul occurs during a running play, the basic enforcement spot is the spot where the run ends (2-25-9) (See Figures 2 and 4).

PLAY. K-1's punt is caught by R-1. During the run, R-1 flag guards at R's 22. R-1 is then deflagged by K-1 at R's 40. **RULING.** Penalize R 10 yards from R's 22, which is the spot of the foul, R's ball 1st and 8 on R's 12. Once the punt is caught, the loose ball play has ended. It is now a running play. The foul by the offensive team behind the basic spot, the end of the run, is enforced from the spot of the foul.

PLAY. K-1's punt is caught by R-1. During the run, K-2 illegally contacts R-1 at K's 35. R-1 is deflagged/tagged at K's 28. **RULING.** Penalize K 10 yards from K's 28, which is the end of the run, R's ball 1st and goal on K's 18. All fouls, except by the offense behind the end of the run, are penalized from the basic spot, the end of the run.

PLAY. Third and 2 on A's 38. QB A-1 runs 2 yards beyond A's scrimmage line (1st ball spotter–orange) and throws an illegal forward pass from A's 40. **RULING.** Fourth and 5 on A's 35. All illegal forward passes are treated as running plays. Penalize from the spot where the pass was thrown, the end of the run.

Basic Enforcement Spots

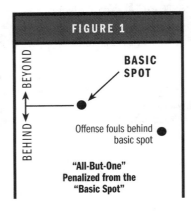

FIGURE 1

BEYOND / BEHIND

BASIC SPOT

Offense fouls behind basic spot

**"All-But-One"
Penalized from the
"Basic Spot"**

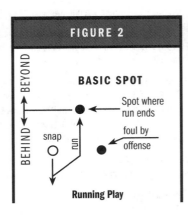

FIGURE 2

BEYOND / BEHIND

BASIC SPOT

Spot where run ends

snap / run

foul by offense

Running Play

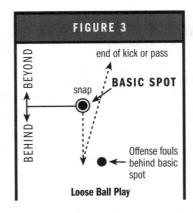

FIGURE 3

BEYOND / BEHIND

end of kick or pass

snap

BASIC SPOT

Offense fouls behind basic spot

Loose Ball Play

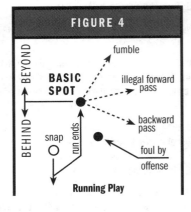

FIGURE 4

BEYOND / BEHIND

fumble

BASIC SPOT

illegal forward pass

backward pass

snap / run ends

foul by offense

Running Play

PLAY. Third and 5 on A's 35. QB A-1 throws a legal forward pass to receiver A-2, who runs to B's 19 and flag guards. A-2 scores an apparent touchdown. **RULING.** No touchdown. Penalize A 10 yards from B's 19, 1st and 9 on B's 29. Once A-2 caught the pass, it became a running play. Since there was a foul by the offense behind the end of the run, which is the goal line, penalize from the spot of the foul.

Section 3. Special Enforcements

Article 1. Automatic 1st Down Fouls.

Fouls by B that give A an automatic 1st down (S8) are Roughing the Passer and Tampering with the Flag Belt.

Article 2. Dead Ball Fouls.

Penalties for dead ball fouls are enforced separately and in the order of occurrence. Dead ball fouls are not coupled with live ball fouls or other dead ball fouls to create double or multiple fouls. Where there are 10 yard dead ball fouls (or live ball fouls treated as dead ball fouls) committed by each team prior to penalty administration, each 10 yard foul will cancel a 10 yard foul on the other team. Any remaining 10 yard fouls will be enforced. Any 5 yard dead ball fouls will be enforced separately and in order of occurrence and would never cancel with a 10 yard foul.

PLAY. After an incomplete pass on 3rd down, B-1 taunts A-2, and A-2 retaliates by shoving B-1. **RULING.** B-1 is guilty of unsportsmanlike conduct, and A-2 is guilty of a dead ball personal foul. Those penalties cancel each other out, and it will be 4th down at the previous spot.

PLAY. Third down and goal at B's 10. After B-1 breaks up a pass intended for A-2, B-1 taunts A-2, and A-2 retaliates by punching B-1. After seeing the covering official's flag, B-3 taunts A-2. **RULING.** The penalty for B-1's unsportsmanlike conduct foul is cancelled out by A-2's dead ball personal foul for fighting. A-2 is disqualified. B-3's penalty is enforced half the distance to the goal. It will be 4th and goal at B's 5. **NOTE:** Even though the yardage penalties for these fouls cancel each other out, the fouls count toward both the disqualification of the involved players and the overall team total toward a forfeit.

Article 3. Double Foul.

It is a double foul if both teams commit fouls (other than unsportsmanlike or nonplayer) during the same down in which

A. there is no change of team possession,

B. there is a change of team possession and the team in possession at the end of the down fouls prior to the final change of possession, or

C. there is a change of team possession and the team in final possession accepts the penalty for its opponent's foul.

In (A), (B), and (C), the penalties cancel and the down is replayed.

EXCEPTION 1: If each team fouls during a down in which there is a change of team possession, the team last gaining possession may retain the ball, provided its foul is not prior to the final change of team possession and it declined the penalty for its opponents foul(s) (other than unsportsmanlike or nonplayer). This exception is commonly referred to as the principle of "clean hands." NOTE: This Rule does not apply to double fouls during a Try or overtime period. EXCEPTION 2: PSK foul. R must decline the K fouls (other than unsportsmanlike or nonplayer).

PLAY. K-1 punts, R-1 catches the ball and throws an illegal forward pass from R's 26. R-2 catches the pass and K-2 holds R-2 prior to the tag/deflag. **RULING.** The Referee will present the following options to the R captain: (1) if you accept the holding foul by K-2, it is a double foul, and the ball will be punted again, if elected; (2) if you want to keep the ball, you must decline the holding foul by K-2. The Referee will mark off 5 yards to R's 21 for the illegal forward pass, R's ball, 1st and 19.

PLAY. A 2nd and goal on B's 6. B-1 intercepts A-1's pass in B's end zone. On the return, B-1 flag guards in B's end zone and A-2 holds on B's 10. B-1 is deflagged/tagged at B's 12. **RULING.** Fouls offset and the down is replayed. (If B declines A's penalty, it would be a safety.)

Article 4. Goal Line.
For a defensive team foul, if the enforcement spot, which is now the basic spot, is on or behind the offended team's goal line, any measurement is from the succeeding spot or goal line.

PLAY. B intercepts a pass in B's end zone, A commits an illegal contact foul, and B then is deflagged/tagged in the end zone. **RULING.** Options for B: either decline the illegal contact foul and accept a touchback, 1st and 6 on B's 14, or accept the illegal contact foul and it will be 1st and 16 on B's 24, enforced from the succeeding spot, B's 14.

PLAY. A 3rd and 14 on A's 6. Passer A-1 runs back into their end zone. B-1 commits illegal contact. B-2 then deflags A-2 in A's end zone. **RULING.** A 3rd and 10 on A's 10. Enforce at goal line.

PLAY. B-1 intercepts a pass in B's end zone. B-3 commits an illegal contact foul after the interception on B's 5 yard line. **RULING.** B's ball, 1st and 17 1/2 on B's 2 1/2. The basic spot on a touchback is the 14. Penalize from B's 5.

Article 5. Half the Distance.
A measurement cannot take the ball more than half the distance from the enforcement spot to the offending team's goal line. If the penalty is greater than this, the ball is placed halfway between the enforcement spot and the goal line.

PLAY. Second and 15 at A's 5. QB A-1 crosses the A's scrimmage line and throws a forward pass from: (a) A's 12 or (b) A's 8. The pass is incomplete. **RULING.** In both cases, the penalty is enforced from the spot of the foul. In (a), it shall be 3rd and 13 at A's 7. In (b), it shall be 3rd and 16 at A's 4.

Article 6. Last Play of 4th Period or Overtime.

Succeeding spot fouls that occur: (a) during the last play of the game or (b) during the last play of an overtime period; or (c) dead ball fouls that occur after the last play of a game or overtime period can be carried over to overtime, unless a touchdown is scored on that play, in which case the penalty can only be enforced on the Try.

PLAY. Score: A-13, B-21. As time expires in the 4th period, A-1 scores touchdown and B-1 roughs the passer. Score is now A-19, B-21. **RULING.** Roughing the passer penalty must be enforced on the Try since overtime might not be played. Same ruling if score was tied.

Article 7. Loss of Down Fouls.

Loss of down (S9) fouls by A: Illegal Backward Pass, Illegal Forward Pass, Intentional Grounding, and Tampering with the Flag Belt.

Article 8. Multiple Foul.

When 2 or more live ball fouls (other than unsportsmanlike or nonplayer) are committed during the same down by the same team, only 1 penalty may be chosen by the offended team.

PLAY. Third and 4 at B's 24. During the play, B is flagged for pass interference, and A receives an Unsportsmanlike Conduct penalty for having illegal player equipment. The pass is incomplete. **RULING.** Penalties for live ball pass interference and dead ball unsportsmanlike conduct are enforced. It will be 1st and 4 at B's 24.

Article 9. Safety.

If the offensive team throws an illegal forward pass from its end zone or commits any other foul for which the penalty is accepted and measurement is from on or behind its goal line, which is now the basic spot, it is a safety.

PLAY. A-1 flag guards and is then deflagged in their end zone. **RULING.** Safety.

Article 10. Touchdown.

A. If there is a foul by the scoring team (other than unsportsmanlike or nonplayer) during a down that results in a touchdown, the acceptance of the penalty nullifies the score.

B. If an opponent of the scoring team commits a foul (other than unsportsmanlike or nonplayer) during a down in which a touchdown is scored, and there was not a change of team possession during the down, A may accept the results of the play and then choose to have the foul enforced either on the Try or after the Try, at the succeeding spot.

C. If an opponent of the scoring team commits a foul (other than unsportsmanlike or nonplayer) during a down in which a touchdown is scored and there was a change of team possession during the down, and such foul occurs after the change of team possession, the scoring team may accept the results of the play and then choose to have the foul enforced either on the Try or after the Try, at the succeeding spot.

D. If either team commits an unsportsmanlike or nonplayer foul during the down in which a touchdown is scored, the opponent may accept the results of the play and then choose to have the foul enforced either on the Try or after the Try, at the succeeding spot.

NOTE: In (B), (C), and (D) above, unless moved by penalty, the succeeding spot will be the 14 yard line or the 10 yard line in overtime.

PLAY. Third and goal on B's 6. QB A-1 runs for a touchdown. B-1 illegally contacts A-3 prior to the touchdown on B's 2. **RULING.** Touchdown. The Referee will ask the A captain or coach whether they wish to go for a 1, 2, or 3 point Try, after explaining that the 10 yard penalty will be enforced as part of the Try or at the 14 yard line. Once the A captain makes a decision, penalize B 10 yards or half the distance on the Try from A's 3, 10, or 20 yard line, if A chose that option.

Article 11. Try.
A. If either team commits a dead ball foul following a touchdown and prior to the initial ready for play on a Try, the offended team has the option of enforcing the penalty on the Try or after the Try, at the succeeding spot.
B. If there is a foul by A (other than unsportsmanlike or nonplayer) during a down that results in a successful Try, acceptance of the penalty nullifies the score. If the foul carries a loss of down, the Try is not replayed.
C. If there is a foul by B during a successful Try, the penalty may be enforced at the succeeding spot.
D. If a double foul occurs, the down is replayed.

PLAY. QB A-1 scores a touchdown and then spikes the ball. **RULING.** The touchdown counts. Initially the Referee will ask the B captain or head coach whether they want the unsportsmanlike foul enforced on either the Try or the succeeding spot. Then the Referee will ask the A captain or head coach whether they want to go for a 1, 2, or 3 point Try. Once the A captain or head coach makes a decision, penalize A 10 yards on the Try from B's 3, 10, or 20 yard line, if B chose that option.

PLAY. Try. QB A-1 runs across B's goal line for a successful 2 point Try. B-1 grabs and holds A-1's jersey in an unsuccessful attempt to deflag A-1. **RULING.** Score 2 points for A. Penalize B half the distance for holding at the succeeding spot, B's 14. It will be 1st and 13 at B's 7.

Article 12. Fouls by K During Punts.
When K fouls during a punt (other than Kick Catching Interference or Illegally Consuming Time), R may have the penalty enforced at either the previous spot or the succeeding spot, provided K will not be next to put the ball in play.

FOULS AND PENALTIES SUMMARY

		Page	Rule	Section	Article	Official's Signal
Loss of 5 Yards						
1.	Failure to Wear Required Player Equipment	25	1	4	5	23
2.	Delay of Game (Dead Ball)	39	3	5		7, 21
3.	Illegally Consuming Time	39	3	6		19
4.	Illegal Substitution	40	3	7	1, 2	22
5.	Illegal Procedure	46	6	1	3, 4	19
6.	Encroachment (Dead Ball)	49	7	2	1	7, 18
7.	False Start (Dead Ball)	49	7	2	2	7, 19
8.	Illegal Snap (Dead Ball)	49	7	2	3	7, 19
9.	Disconcerting Act (Dead Ball)	50	7	2	4	7, 23
10.	Illegal Formation	50	7	3	1, 4	19
11.	Illegal Motion	50	7	3	3	20
12.	Illegal Shift	50	7	3	5	20
13.	**Illegal Advancement (Co-Rec)**	51	7	5		19
14.	Illegal Backward Pass (Loss of Down)	51	7	6	1	35, 9
15.	Illegal Forward Pass (Loss of Down if by A Prior to a Change of Possession)	53	7	7	2A-D	35, 9
16.	Intentional Grounding (Loss of Down)	53	7	7	2E	36, 9
17.	**Illegal Reception: Man to Man Forward Pass Completion on a Closed Play (Loss of Down) (Co-Rec)**	54	7	7	3	19, 9
18.	Help the Runner	66	9	4	4	44
Loss of 10 Yards						
1.	Unsportsmanlike Conduct, Illegal Player Equipment	26	1	6		27
2.	Illegal Kick, Quick Punt	46	6	1	1	31
3.	Kick Catching Interference	47	6	2		33
4.	Two or More Encroachment Fouls During the Interval Between Downs	49	7	2	1	7, 18
5.	Offensive Pass Interference	55	7	10	2	33
6.	Defensive Pass Interference	56	7	10	3	33
7.	Unsportsmanlike Conduct	61	9	1	1-3	27
8.	Personal Foul, Strip or Attempt to Strip the Ball	63	9	3	1A	38
9.	Personal Foul, Throw Runner to the Ground	63	9	3	1B	38

(continued)

FOULS AND PENALTIES SUMMARY *(CONTINUED)*

		Page	Rule	Section	Article	Official's Signal
Loss of 10 Yards *(continued)*						
10.	Personal Foul, Hurdle any Player	63	9	3	1C	38
11.	Personal Foul, Contact Before or After the Ball Is Dead	63	9	3	1D	38
12.	Personal Foul, Unnecessary Contact of any Nature	63	9	3	1E	38
13.	Personal Foul, Drive or Run Into an Opponent	63	9	3	1F	38
14.	Personal Foul, Position Upon Shoulders or Body of a Teammate	63	9	3	1G	38
15.	Personal Foul, Nonplayer Contact with Official in Restricted Area	63	9	3	1J	38
16.	Roughing the Passer (Automatic 1st Down)	64	9	3	2	34, 8
17.	Personal Foul, Illegal Contact	64	9	3	3,4	38
18.	Personal Foul, Interlocked Blocking	64	9	3	5	38, 44
19.	**Illegal Flag Belt Removal**	65	9	4	1C	38
20.	**Guarding the Flag Belt**	65	9	4	2	24
21.	Personal Foul, Illegal Contact	66	9	4	3	38
22.	Holding	66	9	4	5	42
23.	Illegal Batting	66	9	5	1, 2	31
24.	Illegal Kicking	66	9	5	3	31
25.	Illegal Participation	67	9	6		28
Disqualification Associated With Certain 10 Yard Penalties						
1.	**Personal Foul, Tampering with the Flag Belt (Loss of Down if by A) (Automatic 1st Down if by B)**	57, 65	8,9	4,4	1,1E	38, 47 8, 9
2.	Flagrant Unsportsmanlike Conduct	61	9	1	1-3	27, 47
3.	Unsportsmanlike Conduct, Intentionally Contacting an Official	61	9	1	3F	27, 47
4.	Unsportsmanlike Conduct, Leaving the Team Box and Entering the Field During a Fight	61	9	1	3G	27, 47
5.	Flagrant Personal Fouls	63	9	3	1	38, 47
6.	Personal Foul, Tackling the Runner	63	9	3	1H	38, 47
7.	Personal Foul, Fighting an Opponent	63	9	3	1I	38, 47
8.	**Personal Foul, Nonplayer Deflagging or Interfering With a Runner**	65	9	4	1F	38, 5, 47

SPECIAL OLYMPICS UNIFIED FLAG FOOTBALL – COLLEGIATE LEVEL RULES

Introduction to Unified Sports

The mission of Special Olympics is to provide year-round sports training and athletic competition in a variety of Olympic-type sports for children and adults with intellectual disabilities, giving them continuing opportunities to develop physical fitness, demonstrate courage, experience joy, and participate in a sharing of gifts, skills, and friendship with their families, other Special Olympics athletes, and the community. Special Olympics is also dedicated to promoting social inclusion through shared sports training and competition experiences. One of the more effective vehicles for promoting social inclusion is through Special Olympics Unified Sports®, which joins people with and without intellectual disabilities on the same team.

Special Olympics Unified Sports is an inclusive sports program that combines an approximately equal number of Special Olympics athletes (individuals with intellectual disabilities) and Unified partners (individuals without intellectual disabilities) on teams for training and competition. Unified Sports can be offered in team sports such as basketball, flag football, soccer, and volleyball and in other sports such as bocce, golf, and tennis. Successful Unified Sports programs include a number of criteria, including meaningful inclusion for athletes and Unified partners as well as appropriate sport selection.

In partnership with NIRSA: Leaders in Collegiate Recreation, hundreds of colleges are providing Unified Sports intramural leagues on campus. These leagues are inspired by a simple principle: training, playing, and competing together is a quick path to friendship, understanding, and meaningful inclusion. On these campuses, Unified Sports teams are made up of people of similar age and ability, making games more competitive, exciting, and fun for all. Unified Sports intramural leagues welcome Special Olympics athletes, whether students or from the community, and student Unified partners at any level of skill or experience.

In addition to Unified Sports intramural leagues, Special Olympics athletes and Unified partners also have the opportunity to participate in Unified Sports extramural events at the state, regional, and national levels through Special Olympics or the NIRSA Championship Series.

For more information or to learn how to bring Special Olympics Unified Sports intramural leagues to a campus, please visit www.specialolympics.org/our-work/unified-schools/college.

For more information on Special Olympics North America (SONA), please visit www.specialolympics.org/our-work/sports/unified-sports.

Special Olympics Unified Flag Football Rules

This section covers the differences between Special Olympics North America (SONA) and NIRSA flag football rules. SONA flag football rules are the prescribed rules of play for Unified Sports competitions taking place at NIRSA Championship Series flag football tournaments. To see full versions of SONA Unified Sports rules and resources, including flag football, please visit https://resources.specialolympics.org/sports-essentials/sports-and-coaching.

Special Olympics Unified flag football is intended to be noncontact. Rules are made with player safety as the primary consideration. Special Olympics athletes, Unified partners, and any nonplaying members of the team are to be held to the same standard as any other NIRSA competition and should not display unsportsmanlike conduct or act in a disrespectful manner to opponents, officials, and event staff.

One of the main principles of Special Olympics Unified Sports is the Principle of Meaningful Involvement. Meaningful involvement means that each player on the roster is afforded an opportunity to contribute, in both role and playing time, to their team and the outcome of the game in a way that highlights their own unique skill set. Since each player does have a unique skill set, meaningful involvement can be different for each individual player.

Unified Flag Football Rules Differences

These rule differences should be implemented for Unified Sports competitions in intramural play and at the NIRSA Championship Series flag football tournaments. Anything not listed in the SONA Unified Flag Football Rulebook should be played according to the NIRSA Flag & Touch Football Rules Book.

NOTE: It is recognized that some institutions may choose to modify some of the following rules (e.g., field dimensions or roster size) or incorporate any or all of the NIRSA flag football rules for their Unified divisions in order to facilitate play on their campus. If choosing to play predominately under NIRSA flag football rules, teams shall still be composed of both Special Olympics athletes and Unified partners with as close to a 1-to-1 ratio as possible.

1. **Field Dimensions.** SONA Unified flag football is played on a field with smaller dimensions than a standard NIRSA competition. The field is similar to a 4v4 field but with additional no-run zones and a width that is 5 yards smaller.
   A. The field is 60 yards from end line to end line and 25 yards from sideline to sideline.
   B. End zones are 10 yards in length, and there is a 20 yard distance from the goal line to midfield. During play, the two lines to gain will be the midfield line and the goal line.
   C. There are no-run zones marked 5 yards before midfield and before the end zone. When the line of scrimmage is in a no-run zone (including exactly 5 yards before the line to gain), the plays must have a legal forward pass for the offensive team to gain yardage. Teams cannot advance the ball past the line of scrimmage while running, even if a legal handoff occurred. NOTE: The no-run zone is only enforced when the offensive team is within 5 yards of the line to gain.

Diagram of Flag Football Field

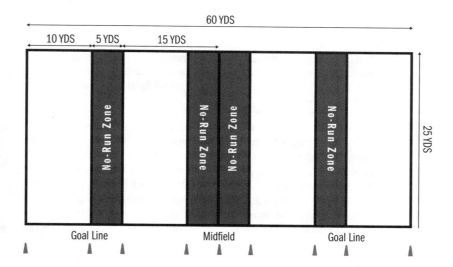

2. **Team Composition.** The teams on the playing field consist of 5 players, with a ratio of 3 athletes and 2 Unified partners. Teams must start a game with 3 athletes and 2 Unified partners. Teams can continue a game with 4 players. At no point can a team play with more Unified partners than athletes.

3. **Scoring.** Touchdown: 6 points. Extra point: 1 or 2 points. Safety: 2 points. Extra point option: 1 point from the 6 yard line; 2 points from the 12 yard line.

4. **Overtime.** If the score is tied at the end of regulation, a coin toss is used to determine first possession of overtime. Each team receives 2 plays from midfield, and the team with the most points scored or yardage gained wins the game. If the team with first possession scores a touchdown on their first play, then the opposing team must do the same on their first play. A team who intercepts a pass wins the game.

5. **Possessions.**

    A.   All possessions, except following an interception, start at the offensive team's 5 yard line. After an interception, the ball changes possession and is placed at the point of the interception. (Interceptions cannot be returned.) An interception in the end zone is placed at the 5 yard line.

    B.   The offense has 4 plays to cross midfield; provided they cross midfield, they will be awarded another 4 plays to score a touchdown. If the offensive team fails to cross midfield or score a touchdown in the prescribed number of plays, possession of the ball changes, and the opposite team starts at their 5 yard line. There are no punts.

C.   Dead balls: The play is dead and marked at the spot of the ball when the ball carrier loses their flag belt (even if the flag belt falls off inadvertently—there is no 1 hand touch), a receiver catches the ball without their flag belt on, or an interception occurs (blow the play dead immediately).

6. Offensive Considerations.

A.   Running the ball: The quarterback is the first person gaining possession of the snap. The quarterback cannot advance the ball past the line of scrimmage as a runner at any time. Only direct handoffs are allowed behind the line of scrimmage. A player receiving a handoff can attempt a pass, as long as they are still behind the line of scrimmage during the attempted pass. A handoff can occur with any combination of athlete/Unified partner behind the line of scrimmage, with the player receiving the handoff eligible to advance the ball. Direct snaps are permitted; the quarterback does not have to be 2 yards back. Diving is not permitted to gain yardage.

B.   Passing/receiving the ball: All passes, including shovel passes, must be forward and received beyond the line of scrimmage to be considered legal. A Unified partner cannot complete a pass to another Unified partner. Backward passes (laterals or pitches) are illegal regardless of field location.

7. Defensive Considerations.
All players who attempt to rush the quarterback must be a minimum of 7 yards from the line of scrimmage when the ball is snapped. A dot or marker is used to designate the 7 yard spot. (The 1 yard defensive line of scrimmage cone is not needed for Unified.) Players *not* rushing the quarterback may be on the line of scrimmage. The 7 yard zone no longer exists once the quarterback makes a handoff. Diving is not permitted to pull flag belts. Defensive players are not required to wear flag belts.

8. Penalties.
All penalties are assessed from the line of scrimmage. A penalty prior to the snap is 5 yards and replay the down. An offensive penalty after the snap is 5 yards and a loss of down. A defensive penalty after the snap is 5 yards and an automatic first down. An unsportsmanlike conduct penalty is 10 yards.

YOUTH FOOTBALL RULES SUMMARY

1-2-3   **Field Markings.** The width of the field should be lined at 15 yard intervals from goal line to goal line. NOTE: The field measures 60 yards in length, goal line to goal line, and 40 yards in width. This Rule applies to U8, U10, and U12 only.

1-2-6   **Team Box.** The team area shall be located 2 yards from the sideline and between the 15 yard lines. This Rule applies to U8, U10, and U12 only.

1-3-1   **Ball Specifications.** The regular, intermediate, youth, junior, or pee wee size football shall be used for youth games.

3-1-4   **Putting the Ball in Play.** The ball shall be placed at A's 10 yard line to begin each half of a game and following a Try, touchback, or safety, unless moved by penalty. NOTE: There are no kickoffs. This Rule applies to U8, U10, and U12 only. U14 leagues will place the ball on A's 14 yard line.

6-1-2   **Punt.** Prior to marking the ball ready for play on 4th down, the Referee must ask the A captain if they want to turn over possession of the football to B. If the A captain responds yes, the Referee will inform the B captain and then mark off 20 yards in advance of the scrimmage line. It will be 1st down for B. There are no punts. This Rule applies to U8 and U10 only.

7-3-4   **Receiving the Snap.** The snap may be 1st touched by an A player at any distance behind A's scrimmage line (1st ball spotter–orange). Direct snaps are legal.

NOTE: U8 players are age 8 and under, U10 players are age 10 and under, etc. These Rules apply to players age 14 and under only.

Youth Field Diagram

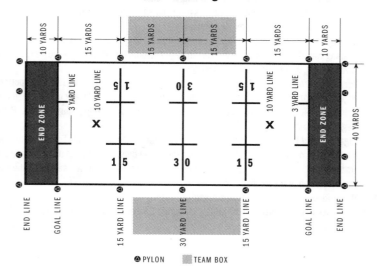

⬤ PYLON   ▨ TEAM BOX

4 ON 4 FOOTBALL RULES SUMMARY

1-1-2   **The Game.** The game shall be played between 2 teams of 4 players each. 3 players are required to avoid a forfeit.

1-2-3   **Field Markings.** The field measures 40 yards in length, goal line to goal line, and 30 yards in width. There shall be 1 hash mark dividing the field into halves.

3-1-1   **Coin Toss.** The captain winning the toss shall select offense, defense, direction, or defer the choice to the 2nd half.

3-1-4   **Putting the Ball in Play.** The ball shall be placed at A's 10 yard line to begin each half of a game and following a Try, touchback, or safety, unless moved by penalty. NOTE: There are no kicks.

3-2-1   **Game Time.** Playing time shall be 2 halves of 12 minutes in length.

3-2-5   **First 11 Minutes.** The clock will start on the snap to begin each half. It will run continuously for the first 11 minutes unless stopped by a team or Referee's time-out.

3-2-6   **1 Minute Warning.** Approximately 1 minute before the end of each half the Referee shall stop the clock and inform both captains of the playing time remaining in the half. The clock starts on the snap.

3-2-7   **Last 1 Minute.** A start, stop clock shall be used.

3-3-3   **Tie Breaker.** Each team will attempt to score by passing from the 3 yard line for 1 point, from the 10 yard line for 2 points, or from the 20 yard line for 3 points.

3-4-3   **Charged Time-Outs.** Each team is entitled to 2 charged time-outs per game, including overtimes.

5-1-2   **Series of Downs.** Each team shall have 3 consecutive downs to advance the ball to the next zone by scrimmage.

5-1-4   **A New Series of Downs.** A new series of downs is awarded when a team moves the ball legally into the next zone or the opponent obtains team possession of the ball by penalty, pass interception, or failure to advance to the next zone.

Rule 6   **Kicking the Ball.** All kicks are illegal. *Penalty:* Illegal Kicking, 5 yards (S31).

Rule 7   **Rushing the QB.** B cannot cross their scrimmage line until the pass is released. *Penalty:* Illegal Advancement, 3 yards from the previous spot (S19).

7-5-1   **Runner.** An A runner cannot advance the ball through A's scrimmage line (1st ball spotter-orange). There are no restrictions (A) once the ball has been touched by any player beyond the A scrimmage line, (B) after a change of team possession, or (C) after a legal forward pass. *Penalty:* Illegal Advancement, 3 yards (S19).

7-7-1   **Legal Forward Pass.** There must be a legal forward pass each down. A has 5 seconds to release the ball on a forward pass. If A fails to release the ball in time, it is a loss of down and the ball is next snapped at the previous spot. The Referee will sound their whistle at 5 seconds if the passer has possession of the football.

8-3-1   **Mercy Rule.** The Mercy Rule does not apply.

Rule 10   **Enforcement of Penalties.** All 10 yard penalties are 5 yards and all 5 yard penalties are 3 yards.

4 on 4 Field Diagram

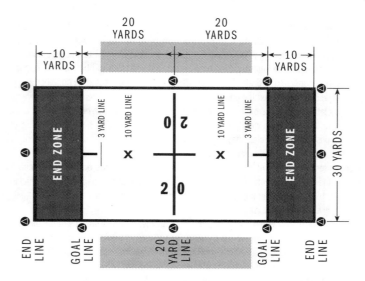

10 COMMANDMENTS FOR CLINICIANS AND OBSERVERS

Keep these important guidelines in mind when evaluating, observing, and teaching:

1. **Be Fair and Impartial.** We all know many officials we are watching. That should not, and cannot, affect our opinions and evaluations. We are doing a disservice to the players, coaches, officials, and even our friends we are observing when we are not honest and fair. We must be above reproach.

2. **We Do Not Know All the Answers.** Find out why they did what they did before criticizing them for it. Find out what happened and why. Then offer suggestions on how it could be done better.

3. **Be Constructive.** Remember the purpose of an observer is, first and foremost, to improve the quality of the officiating. Also, remember that the only way your comments can help an official to improve is if you share the comments with the official. Approach each official at halftime and after the game, whenever possible. Our officials may be learning the game for the 1st time, so be patient, calm, and answer all their questions, if possible.

4. **Be Consistent.** We really need to do our best to evaluate everyone on the same scale and give everyone the same information. The most frustrating thing that can happen to an official is when 1 observer tells them something in 1 game, and in the next game they are told something just the opposite by a different observer.

5. **Think Big Picture First When Observing.** Too often observers nitpick officials rather than look at the major officiating fundamentals—initial position, read and react then flow, communication with fellow officials and players, dead ball officiating, and so on. Concentrate on the major items first. Then be specific—explain in some detail what happened and how it can be corrected.

6. **Be Discreet With Your Constructive Comments.** Our criticisms should be shared with the crew but not with other officials. We should be a positive influence on the program and should not criticize officials to other officials or in front of players, coaches, or spectators.

7. **Praise at Least 3 Times as Much as You Criticize.** We all know people respond better to positive comments than to negative comments, so whenever possible, cast even your criticism in a positive manner, perhaps by praising someone else on the crew as a means of pointing out to another crew member a better way to do it.

8. **Don't Be Afraid to Say I Do Not Know.** Often we are asked what we thought about a particular play, whether the pass was caught, what the proper mechanic or Rule is, or what happened on a particular play. And often we do not know. Admit it when you do not know. If it is a Rule or mechanic addressed in the *NIRSA Rules Book and Officials' Manual*, determine the correct answer and follow up with the official.

9. **Be Careful When Judging Fouls From the Sideline.** Our job as observers is primarily "mechanics oriented" rather than "penalty oriented." We will occasionally be able to comment on a foul that was called, but normally we will not see it or we will not get nearly as good a look at it as the official got.

10. **Don't Forget What It Is Like to Be on the Field.** Remember how quickly things happen on the field. Remember the angles on the field are different and people can be screened or distracted by other action.

NIRSA FOOTBALL OFFICIALS' MANUAL

This *NIRSA Football Officials' Manual* has been designed to give officials detailed information regarding officiating mechanics. Through evaluation and study, the techniques presented are recognized and accepted as officiating standards wherever flag and touch football are played.

The following positions are used throughout the manual:

> 3-Person Crew: Referee (R), Line Judge (LJ), and Back Judge (BJ)
> 4-Person Crew: Referee (R), Line Judge (LJ), Field Judge (FJ), and Back Judge (BJ)

The following team designations are used throughout the manual:

> Team A (A) is the team that snaps the ball.
> Team B (B) is the opponent of Team A.
> Team K (K) is the team that legally kicks the ball.
> Team R (R) is the opponent of Team K.

The manual is broken up into seven parts:

> Part I. Officiating Basics
> Part II. Game Administration
> Part III. Officiating Responsibilities
> Part IV. Communication
> Part V. 3-Person Mechanics
> Part VI. 4-Person Mechanics
> Part VII. NIRSA Official Flag Football Signals

Ultimately, the official serves two primary purposes: to protect the safety of the participants and to protect the integrity of the game. Football is a difficult sport to officiate and will present many challenging situations during each game. When an official is faced with a situation that causes doubt, using safety and fairness as guiding principles will usually result in a correct decision being made.

The officiating mechanics detailed within this manual are intended to be general guidelines for officials to use when working a game. Although these mechanics will almost always put officials in the best position to succeed, this manual will never be able to address every single situation that is presented to officials. Officials must use common sense and adapt to game situations to enable them to officiate in the best interest of the game.

PART I. OFFICIATING BASICS

Section 1. Foundations of Officiating

Article 1. Rules and Mechanics Knowledge.

Knowledge of the rules and officiating mechanics must be excellent and supplemented by the ability to interpret them correctly through much time and study. All rules should be enforced fairly and consistently. Enforce the "spirit of the rule" by exercising good common sense. Utilize proper officiating philosophies through the "If in Doubts." Develop a firm understanding of the officiating duties of each position and how the positions function together.

Article 2. Integrity.

Officials are charged with upholding the integrity of the game; thus, honesty and neutrality are essential. Officials are held to a higher standard, so your actions on and off the field must be above reproach. Do not discuss with a team the play or players of their opponents in a game that you will officiate or are officiating. Do not get mad or retaliate against coaches or players who disagree with your calls. Always work hard no matter what the game or who you think may be watching.

Article 3. Appearance and Conditioning.

The appearance of an official is usually the first impression made on players, coaches, and fans regarding the ability of that official. Thus, officials must present themselves in a manner that demonstrates that they are prepared for the job at hand. Wear a complete uniform that is clean and fits properly. Stay well-groomed, as maintaining a professional appearance is critical to establishing credibility. Take positive steps toward creating and maintaining good physical condition to assist with your ability to officiate the game properly.

Article 4. Hustle.

Hustle, but do not hurry. Move with a purpose, allowing the play to come to you. Let your mind digest what your eyes have seen. Hustle to a position that allows you to stand still several yards away from the play at the point of judgment (Stop and Watch), giving you the best chance to process the play.

Article 5. Resolve.

There are difficult moments in officiating that force officials to step out of their comfort zone to accomplish what is in the best interest of the game. No matter how big the game or call may appear, be confident and decisive. Trust partner officials, but be prepared to bring information to your partners so that the crew can make the best decision possible.

Section 2. Uniform

Article 1. Shirts.

A short- or long-sleeved shirt with 1" black-and-white vertical stripes, a Byron collar, black cuffs, and a breast pocket. All crew members should have matching sleeve lengths. Undershirts and turtlenecks should be black, with no letters or shapes that can be seen through the shirt. The zipper should be zipped up to or near the very top. Shirts must be completely tucked in.

Article 2. Shorts/Pants/Belt.

Primarily black athletic pants or shorts, or black pants with a 1 1/4" white stripe down each leg. A black belt is to be worn with all pants that have belt loops.

Article 3. Shoes/Socks.

Primarily black athletic shoes or cleats with black laces. Shoes should be clean and polished. Socks should be black.

Article 4. Hat/Gloves.

A black hat with traditional, narrow white piping. Hats should be clean and not discolored. When worn, gloves should be black.

Article 5. Officiating Equipment.

Essential equipment includes

- A. Whistle: A plastic, black, traditional or finger whistle. If a lanyard is worn, it must be black.
- B. Penalty Flag: At least one light-gold penalty flag. Penalty flags should be virtually hidden from view when worn, and are not to be altered.
- C. Bean Bag: A white, blue, or black bean bag to mark non-penalty spots.
- D. Info Card: A card and writing utensil to record pertinent information.
- E. Down Indicator: A black, elastic down indicator or other device to keep track of downs.
- F. Watch: An electronic countdown-style watch with a black band.
- G. Coin: A flipping coin to conduct the coin toss.

Section 3. Using the Officiating Equipment

Article 1. Use of Game Card.

Game cards are necessary for officials to record essential data throughout the game. The following information should be recorded throughout the game:

- A. The names and numbers of the team captains and/or head coaches.
- B. The results of the coin toss, including the winner of the toss, the choice of each team, and whether the choice was deferred to the second half.
- C. The time on the clock when each time-out is called, along with which player or coach called the time-out.
- D. All scores, including the time on the clock at the time of each score.
- E. All unsportsmanlike conduct and disqualification fouls, including any applicable numbers of players or names of coaches.

Article 2. Use of Whistle.

While the ball is live, officials should keep the whistle out of their mouth until the ball becomes dead by Rule. The whistle does not kill the play, rather it is used to signify that the play is already dead. Do not be in a hurry to sound your whistle. One strong blast should be used to signify that the play is over. Multiple short blasts should be used to get the attention of the players or of the officials' crew.

Article 3. Use of Watch.

The R is responsible for timing the play clock. The BJ is responsible for timing the game clock. Both responsibilities must be done using an electronic watch to ensure accuracy and consistency. Officials must still utilize vocal communication with the teams to inform them of clock statuses, especially in games where there is no visible scoreboard.

Article 4. Use of Bean Bag.

The bean bag is used to mark potential spots of enforcement. Bean bags should be dropped, not thrown. A bean bag should be used to mark the following spots:

A. The spot where R possesses the punt (Post Scrimmage Kick spot).
B. The spot of 1st touching by K.
C. The spot of possession when the momentum rule is in effect.
D. The spot where a backward pass is intercepted.
E. The spot where a player loses possession when a fumble lands in an opponent's end zone.

Article 5. Use of Hat.

The hat is used to mark where A or K steps out of bounds during a live ball. The hat should be dropped whether or not the player is forced out by an opponent.

If necessary, the hat may also be used to indicate that a dead-ball foul has been committed when the official has already thrown his or her flag. In these scenarios, the hat should be thrown high, in a manner similar to how the official would throw a flag.

PART II. GAME ADMINISTRATION

Section 1. Pregame Duties

Article 1. Officials' Meeting.

It is recommended that officials conduct a pregame meeting to ensure that the crew is on the same page and prepared to officiate the game. Topics of conversation should include, but are not limited to, crew mechanics, communication, rules changes, team tendencies, and conflict management techniques.

Article 2. Field/Equipment Inspection.

It is recommended that officials inspect the field and equipment prior to the game. Hazardous objects and obstructions must be removed from the field.

After inspecting the field, officials should inspect player equipment and resolve any issues before the game. Equipment to inspect should include, but is not limited to, jewelry, pockets, game balls, casts, braces, towels, and flag belts.

Article 3. Captains' and Coaches' Meeting.

Following field and equipment inspection, but prior to the coin toss, officials should meet with each team's head coach and/or captain(s). Officials should introduce themselves and the R should ask the coach/captain(s): "Are your players legally equipped according to the rules?" Inform the coach/captain(s) that the coin toss will occur 3 minutes prior to the start of the game. Other topics of conversation should include, but are not limited to, sporting behavior, new rules, unusual plays, and general questions.

Section 2. Coin Toss

The coin toss shall occur 3 minutes prior to the start of the game.

3-person mechanics: The R shall wait for the captains in the middle of the field. The LJ and BJ shall escort the captains from their respective sidelines upon beckoning from the R.

4-person mechanics: The R and BJ shall wait for the captains in the middle of the field. The LJ and FJ shall escort the captains from their respective sidelines upon beckoning from the R.

Introduce the captains to each other and the officials. The visiting captain calls the toss, informing the R of the call prior to the flip. The R can either catch the coin or let it fall to the ground; however, both teams should know the procedure prior to the flip.

Indicate the winner of the toss by placing your hand on that captain's shoulder. If the winning captain defers the choice until the second half, turn to the press box (or LJ sideline), and give the appropriate signal (S10). Obtain the choice from the captain with the option for the first half. Obtain the other choice from the opposing captain. Place the captains with their backs to the goal they will defend. Indicate which team will begin with the ball by signaling first down (S8). Following the dismissal of the captains, all officials must record the results of the coin toss on their game card.

Section 3. Beginning a Period

All officials must record the down, distance, and yard line nearest the forward point of the ball. The R and LJ should measure the distance from the nearest yard line to the forward point of the ball. The R should estimate the distance from the nearest hash mark to the forward point of the ball. All officials are responsible for ensuring that the ball is placed in the correct location to start the new period.

Section 4. Time-Outs

Article 1. Officials' Time-Out.

Signal the time-out (S3) and tap your chest with your hands. Declare the ball ready for play as soon as the need for the time-out has been met.

Do not stop the clock immediately if in doubt about the nature of an injury. Ask if the injured player can continue, wait for a response, and then assess the situation. Be deliberate and permit as much time as necessary. The safety of the injured player is important. Beckon the coach or game administration onto the field if necessary.

Article 2. Team Time-Out.

All officials may recognize a team time-out and stop the clock using the time-out signal (S3). The official should recognize the time-out by turning to the requesting team with both arms extended and moving both arms 2 times in a horizontal motion toward that team. The R should indicate the time-out by announcing the team that called the time-out and moving both arms 2 times in a horizontal motion toward that team. Also announce the number of the charged time-out for that team for that half.

All officials must record which team called the time-out and the game time when it was called. The R is responsible for timing the time-out. After 45 seconds have elapsed, give multiple short blasts of the whistle to inform the teams that the time-out ends in 15 seconds. Once 60 seconds have elapsed, the R should declare the ball ready for play.

Section 5. Halftime

After the teams return to their sidelines, the BJ should start timing the 5 minute halftime. Prior to declaring the ball ready for play to signify the start of the 2nd half, the R should announce the score.

Section 6. Scoring Plays

Following an apparent touchdown, the covering official must check the legality of the flag belt of the scoring player by pulling off the flag belt of that player. If the official struggles with removing the flag belt, it must first be carefully inspected prior to penalizing the player for illegally securing or tampering with the flag belt. If necessary, the R should also inspect the flag belt before ruling on its legality. The R should not pick up the ball spotters or signal touchdown until after all requirements have been met and there are no penalty flags.

Following a touchdown, the R should use these procedures to administer the Try:

A. Inform team captains or coaches of enforcement options if there is a foul by the opponent of the scoring team, or a foul by either team prior to the declaration of the Try.
B. Ask the scoring team the value of the Try.
C. Reset the ball spotters and announce the administration of the foul(s) and the value of the Try.
D. Once the value of the Try has been announced, it may only be changed if either team calls a time-out. The value of the Try may not be changed if a dead ball foul occurs after the ready for play signal, or if a live ball foul occurs during the Try.

Following the Try, the R should announce the result of the Try, including any penalties that have been enforced at the succeeding spot. Announce the game score and time remaining in the period.

Section 7. Penalty Administration

Article 1. Calling the Foul.

For fouls that have no spot (dead ball, simultaneous with the snap, etc.), throw the flag high above the head to give players and fellow officials a chance to see it. For fouls that have a spot, throw the flag on the corresponding yard line, not toward the players near the spot. If the flag toss is errant, pick up the flag and move it to the appropriate spot of the foul after the play is over. Do not touch or point to the offending player.

Once a foul is called and the ball is declared dead, all officials are responsible for ensuring that the dead ball spot and the spot of the foul are covered. Typically, the non-calling LJ or FJ should cover the dead ball spot, and the non-calling BJ should cover the spot of the foul.

Article 2. Preliminary Signals.

When the ball is declared dead and a foul has occurred, the calling official should give multiple short blasts of the whistle to alert players and officials that a foul has occurred. If a foul occurs during the last 2 minutes of each half, signal time-out (S3) 2 times when the ball is declared dead, then give multiple short blasts.

If only 1 official calls a foul, give the preliminary signal of the type of foul while jogging toward the R to report the foul.

If multiple officials call fouls on the same play, those officials must get together to discuss the foul(s) prior to reporting them to the R. If it is determined that multiple officials called the same foul, move the flags together at the appropriate spot of the foul. Then 1 of the officials can give the preliminary signal of the type of foul while jogging to the R to report the foul.

If it is determined that multiple officials called different fouls, no preliminary signal(s) should be given to the R.

Article 3. Reporting the Foul to the R

All: Prior to communicating the foul, the calling official should report to the R the result of the play. The official(s) calling the foul(s) should report to the R using the 4 Ws:

- A.   What: Type of foul (dead ball or live ball). Describe the foul.
- B.   Who: Offense, defense, kicking team, receiving team.
- C.   When: The status of the ball (loose, in possession, or after a change of team possession).
- D.   Where: The previous spot, the spot where the run ends, or the spot of the foul.

Communicate to the R any special enforcement(s) (half distance to the goal, automatic 1st down, loss of down, succeeding spot enforcements, etc.)

R: When fouls are reported, give the preliminary signal while standing still before explaining options to the coach or captain. You can give the preliminary signal from anywhere on the field; it does not need to be at the ball spotters. Do not give a preliminary signal for delay of game, encroachment, or false start fouls.

Article 4. Determining Options with Coaches and Captains.

R: If the choice is obvious, proceed with enforcement or declination. Otherwise, explain the options to the coach or captain. State options clearly and briefly. Repeat the options if the coach or captain is unsure. Do not engage in conversation with a coach or player about the judgment of the foul until after penalty administration. If there are less than 2 minutes remaining in the game, ask the offended coach or captain if they want the clock to start on the snap, when it would have normally started on the ready. If the choice is obvious, start the clock on the snap.

Article 5. Walking off the Penalty.

All: All officials are responsible for properly enforcing all penalties. Improperly enforcing a penalty is unacceptable and reflects poorly on the entire crew. Correct any mistakes and, if necessary, call an officials' time-out to ensure that the proper result is achieved.

R: Step off the correct yardage and place the ball spotters on the ground 1 yard apart.

LJ: Make sure that the down box is not moved until penalty administration is complete. Step off the correct yardage independent of the R and the FJ.

FJ: Step off the correct yardage independent of the R and the LJ.

BJ: Communicate any special enforcements and clock status as necessary.

Article 6. Final Signals and Announcement.

R: After the penalty is administered and the neutral zone is set, take a position clear of the players and stand still. Give the final signal(s) and announcement facing the LJ side.

- A.   Accepted Penalty: Signal the foul and extend 1 arm in a pointing fashion, horizontally in the direction of the offending team.
- B.   Declined Penalty: Signal the foul and extend 1 arm in a pointing fashion, horizontally in the direction of the offending team. Then give the penalty declined signal (S10).
- C.   Offsetting Penalties: Signal the foul and extend 1 arm in a pointing fashion, horizontally in the direction of the offending team. Repeat this procedure for a foul by the other team. Then give the penalty declined signal (S10).
- D.   No Foul: If there was no foul on the play, signal disregard flag (S13).

While giving the final signal(s), announce the following:
A. When the foul occurred if there was a change of team possession
B. The type of foul
C. Who committed the foul
D. The penalty yardage or declination of the penalty
E. The down and unique information (replay, automatic 1st down, loss of down, etc.)
F. The status of the clock if during the last 2 minutes of the half

Calling Fouls

Stop the clock
for foul

Give preliminary
signal

Indicate offending
team

Give offended
captain or coach
options

Enforce penalty

Repeat penalty
signal

Indicate offending
team

Indicate down

When ball is ready
give "ready for
play" or...

Wind the clock

Section 8. Overtime

Following the conclusion of regulation, the R should call a conference that includes all officials, players, and coaches. Explain the overtime rules and procedures and answer any questions. Excuse everyone but the officials and captains. Conduct a coin toss, with the visiting team calling the toss. This is the only coin toss of overtime. If additional overtime periods are played, the captains will alternate choices.

Section 9. Postgame Duties

Once the R officially ends the game, all officials should exit the field together in a direction that is away from the teams.

PART III. OFFICIATING RESPONSIBILITIES

Section 1. Counting Players

Prior to the start of every down, all officials are responsible for counting the number of players and flag belts to verify the legality of each team. This essential task must be done on every play, regardless of whether or not teams substitute. The R and LJ are responsible for counting A or K players. The BJ and FJ are responsible for counting B or R players. Verify the count with partner officials using the appropriate signal (S17). To prevent unfair play, communicate with players if their team has too many or too few players.

Section 2. Forward Progress and Spotting the Ball

When determining forward progress, mark the forward point of the ball, not the player, when the play becomes dead by rule. Officials should use their downfield foot to indicate this location to the R. Sideline officials should square off spots by moving to the desired spot using a 90 degree angle. This provides a more precise spot while enhancing credibility.

For plays that are standard and do not end near the sideline, officials should come onto the field no more than 5 yards from the sideline when spotting the ball. For plays that end near the sideline, sideline officials should be deliberate when moving to the spot and keep a safe distance that will not interfere with the players. Clean up plays out of bounds by turning to keep the players in view who are out of bounds. Do not turn to face the field until all players have re-entered the field from out of bounds.

Section 3. Setting the Ball Spotters

The LJ is responsible for providing the forward progress spot to the R. If any other official obtains the initial forward progress spot, that official should pass that spot to the LJ. If the ball becomes dead between the hashes, that location is the succeeding spot. If the ball becomes dead outside of the hashes, the nearest hash is the inbounds spot. The intersection of the forward progress spot and the inbounds spot is where the R shall place the ball spotter used to indicate the A scrimmage line. The ball spotter used to indicate the B scrimmage line shall be placed 1 yard downfield. The B scrimmage line may extend into the B end zone.

Section 4. General Signals

Signals are used to communicate information to players, coaches, spectators, and fellow officials. They are the most effective form of nonverbal communication; thus, signals should be given promptly and distinctly. Officials must have a strong knowledge of the Code of Official Football Signals (see page 117) so that communication remains consistent from official to official and crew to crew. Signals should only be given by the covering official(s). Unless giving the time-out signal (S3), officials should never mirror the signal of another official.

Most plays present an obvious result that is immediately understood by the players and officials. Signals during these plays should be smooth and crisp, simply used to acknowledge what everyone already knows. Basic plays such as a spot several yards short of the line-to-gain, or an obvious incomplete pass, should be undemonstrative and represent the nature of the play. Blowing one loud whistle while giving crisp signals is typically enough to effectively communicate the result of the play.

Section 5. Selling the Call

During critical or unusual situations, officials will need to demonstrate their decisiveness when making a call. Selling the call using verbal communication and increased strength of signals lends additional credibility to the call that the official just made. This is especially important in situations where both teams may question the result of the play.

Situations in which to sell a call include, but are not limited to, any of the following:

A. Did the runner cross the line-to-gain, or was the runner stopped short of the line? Yell either "1st down, 1st down" or "short, short."

B. Did the passer release the ball forward, or did the defender deflag/tag the passer first? Either yell "ball's away" or blow your whistle and then yell "flag pulled."

C. Did the runner pass the ball backward, or did the defender deflag/tag the runner first? Either yell and signal "back" or blow your whistle and then yell "flag pulled."

D. Was the ball caught, or did it hit the ground or get trapped first? If caught, give the spot. If the ball hit the ground, signal incomplete and hit the ground with your hand.

E. Was the receiver inbounds near the sideline or end line when controlling the ball, or did he/she step out of bounds in the process? If caught, give the catch signal before spotting the ball. If incomplete because the ball was juggled prior to possession, give the incomplete signal followed by the juggle signal. If incomplete because the ball was caught with a foot on the line, give the incomplete signal followed by a sweeping motion out of bounds.

Section 6. Last 2 Minutes of Each Half

R: At approximately 2 minutes before the end of the 2nd and 4th periods, stop the clock and announce the 2 minute warning. Announce the score and the number of remaining time-outs for each team. Announce the remaining time in the half, and that the clock will start and stop based upon the timing rules.

BJ: You are primarily responsible for loudly announcing the remaining time and whether the clock is running or stopped after every play during the last 2 minutes of the 2nd and 4th periods.

All: During the last 2 minutes of the 2nd and 4th periods, officials should vocally communicate the status of the clock including the time remaining, whether the clock is running or stopped, and if the clock starts on the snap or the ready for play whistle. Using proper signals is important, but also be vocal to keep the players informed.

All: Use the time-out signal (S3) on out-of-bounds plays, penalties, change of team possession, time-outs, and 1st downs. The time-out signal should be given twice and mirrored by all officials. Do not use the time-out signal after giving a signal for touchdown, touchback, safety, or incomplete pass, as these signals already signify that the clock is stopped.

All: When the ball becomes dead inbounds near the sideline but does not gain a first down, give the start clock signal (S2) twice to indicate that the clock should continue to run. This signal should only be used for plays near the sideline.

All: When the ball becomes dead inbounds near the sideline and the runner gained a first down, give the time-out signal (S3) twice to stop the clock. Inform the R whether the clock starts on the ready for play whistle by winding your index finger, or whether the clock starts on the snap by snapping your fingers.

Section 7. Down Box Operation

LJ: Supervise the down box operator. Position the down box a minimum of 6' off the sideline on the line-to-gain for every down, including the Try. During the Try, the down box should display the point value of the Try.

LJ: Verify the preceding down before instructing the operator to change the down box. Inform the down box operator not to move to the next zone line-to-gain until told to do so. Advise the down box operator to move back quickly and out of the way if there is a chance of the play coming toward them. Instruct the down box operator not to drop the down box.

PART IV. COMMUNICATION

Section 1. Communication With Other Officials

Article 1. Pre-Snap Communication.

Most pre-snap communication with other officials occurs nonverbally. Eye contact is important, but utilize your voice if necessary. All officials must verify the down prior to the R declaring the ball ready for play. Verify the count with partner officials using the appropriate signal (S17). If appropriate, communicate whether the clock will start on the snap or ready for play signal.

Article 2. Dual Coverage Areas.

If multiple officials share coverage responsibilities, the official who is primarily responsible should have the first opportunity to make the call. Utilize nonverbal signals (head nods, shaking your head, etc.) to inform the other official(s) of your opinion on the play. If you have definitive knowledge as to the result of the play, be decisive and react accordingly. If you have any doubt, be patient, allowing your partner official(s) the opportunity to provide information or rule on the play.

The FJ is primarily responsible for officiating plays on the line-to-gain or the goal line, so the LJ should give that official the first opportunity to make the call. The FJ should defer to the LJ if the play ends near the intersection of the LJ's sideline and the goal line.

When officiating catches on the sideline, the primary official should officiate "feet first, then ball." This means to first ensure that the receiver's 1st foot down is inbounds, then ensure that the receiver maintains possession of the ball throughout the catch. The sideline official is always responsible for the sideline, and the BJ or R should help the wing official decide if the player maintained possession of the ball.

When officiating catches in the corners of the end zone, the BJ and covering sideline official must first make eye contact to confirm that the receiver's foot was not touching the sideline or end line prior to possessing the ball.

Article 3. Helping with the Call.

If an official recognizes that a rule has been incorrectly applied or a penalty has been incorrectly enforced, that official must step in immediately and help the R correct the situation. It is unacceptable for the crew to misapply a rule or incorrectly enforce a penalty.

If an official makes a judgment call, and another official is convinced with utmost certainty that an error has been made, the non-calling official should provide additional information to the calling official. The helping official should signal for an officials' time-out while moving toward the calling official. The conversation should be brief and the helping official should be decisive in providing information.

Calling officials should recognize when a partner is bringing additional information and be open to using that information to change the call. Ultimately, it is the calling official's decision as to whether the call should be changed.

Section 2. Communication With Players

Article 1. Dead Ball Communication.

At the end of the play, covering officials are responsible for the runner or players directly involved in the action; thus, it is critical for non-covering officials to watch the surrounding players to prevent problems from occurring. Often, players away from the play will engage in poor behavior, so officials must have all players in their collective vision at all times.

Moving toward the players during dead ball times is often enough to announce your presence. However, there will be times when an official will need to utilize their voice or whistle to get the attention of the players. Be firm yet respectful when communicating with players. Be open to answering questions. Always remain positive, direct, and professional.

Article 2. Preventive Communication.

Officials are there to maintain player safety and enforce the spirit of the rules. Although calling fouls is part of the job, officials should do their best to prevent fouls from occurring and allow the game to develop a flow. As such, it is recommended that when an official observes a player about to commit a foul during a dead ball period, that official should offer information to the player or team to prevent the foul.

Preventive communication should occur prior to the snap, not during the play. Examples of preventive communication include, but are not limited to, the following:

All:	A.	Inform teams when they have too many or too few players on the field prior to the snap.
All:	B.	Inform players when they are failing to wear a flag belt or are wearing illegal equipment.
All:	C.	Remind players to tuck in their jerseys and adjust their flag belts if necessary.
R:	D.	Inform the snapper not to snap the ball until the ready for play whistle is blown.
R:	E.	Inform A not to snap the ball until all players have been set for at least 1 second.
R:	F.	Verbalize the status of the play clock, counting down from 5.
LJ:	G.	Inform players who originally line up in the neutral zone to back up behind their scrimmage line.
LJ:	H.	Inform A that the player who receives the snap must first touch the ball at least 2 yards behind the A scrimmage line.
LJ:	I.	Remind players not to enter the neutral zone on punts prior to the ball being kicked.
BJ:	J.	Loudly verbalize the status of the game clock on every play during the last 2 minutes of each half.

Section 3. Communication With Coaches and Captains

The coaches or team captains are leaders of the team and building a strong relationship with them is important to managing a successful game. Thus, communication with coaches and team captains should be more open and professional than communication with general players. Communication with coaches should occur with the coaches remaining in or near their team box.

Present yourself in a strong yet courteous manner that projects composure. Make direct eye contact whenever possible. If a coach or captain asks a question, answer it. If you don't know the answer, get the information from other officials and provide the answer. Coaches or captains will never agree with every call that is made, but they must be afforded respect and treated with professionalism at all times.

Section 4. Communication With Spectators

Officials should refrain from communicating with spectators. Block them out and do not let them take your attention away from the game. If a spectator is creating a dangerous or unpleasant environment, respectfully ask the coach or captain for assistance with the spectator. If necessary, communicate with game administration to resolve the issue and remove the problematic spectator(s).

PART V. 3-PERSON MECHANICS

Section 1. Scrimmage Plays

Article 1. Before the Snap.

All: A.   Initial positions may vary depending upon play situations, team formations, tendencies, field, and weather conditions. Always box in the play, as all players should be in the collective vision of the officiating crew at all times. When in doubt, take a position that is wider and deeper that avoids interfering with the players.

All: B.   Signal and verify the down with other officials. Check the down box for accuracy. Communicate the clock status as necessary. Remind the players to tuck in their jerseys and adjust their flag belts as necessary. Be alert for time-outs, dead ball fouls, injuries, and anything out of the ordinary. Ensure that all officials are in proper position prior to allowing the ball to become live.

R: C.   Take an initial position on the opposite side of the field as the LJ and on the same side as the BJ. Start approximately 7 yards behind and 7 yards wide of the deepest offensive back at a 45 degree angle. Be in a position to see the snap, backs, and players near the snapper. Be alert for false starts and illegal shifts by A. Communicate to A when there are 15 seconds and 10 seconds remaining on the play clock. With 5 seconds remaining on the play clock, count down 5-4-3-2-1 so that the player(s) in position to receive the snap can hear.

R: D.   Upon the conclusion of the previous play, set the ball spotters in the appropriate location on or inside the hash marks to create the neutral zone. Announce the down/distance and mark the ball ready for play by blowing your whistle and giving the appropriate signal (S1). The ready for play procedure and announcement should not prevent a team from snapping the ball quickly. Start timing the play clock upon marking the ball ready for play. Announce "Double Stakes" if A must obtain two lines-to-gain, and "Triple Stakes" for three lines-to-gain.

LJ: E.   Take an initial position between the neutral zone on the sideline opposite the R and BJ. If wide receivers line up near the sideline, or if the line-to-gain or goal line is threatened, start 2 yards off the sideline. Be in a position to see the snap, neutral zone, and players on both sides of the line of scrimmage. Be aware of incoming and exiting substitutes. Be alert for encroachments, false starts, illegal snaps, illegal formations, illegal shifts, and illegal motions. Take responsibility for A players in motion at the snap.

LJ: F.   Upon the conclusion of the previous play, mark the forward progress spot and indicate the next location of the A scrimmage line. Use your downfield foot and raise your arm straight above your head while indicating the next down. Upon giving the R the spot, communicate the next down and distance to the down box.

BJ: G.   Take an initial position on the opposite side of the field as the LJ. Start approximately 20 yards beyond A's scrimmage line, always deeper than the deepest defensive back, and 5 yards from the sideline, always wider than the widest wide receiver. Be aware of incoming and exiting substitutes. Communicate the clock status as necessary.

BJ: H.   Upon the conclusion of the previous play, if necessary, mark the forward progress spot and pass this spot onto the LJ to indicate the next location of the A scrimmage line.

Article 2. Reading and Understanding Keys.

All: A.   Keys are intended to help determine officials' coverage areas at the initial snap. Officials must be prepared to react to the play as it develops. Keys do not necessarily determine coverage for the entire play, as constant adjustments are necessary.

All: B.   Officials should become familiar with the concept of "player, zone, ball." Player refers to the initial key(s) that the official should focus on at the snap. As the play develops, officials should switch to covering a zone of the field that could impact the play. Once the offense commits to passing or running into a specific zone, covering officials should focus their attention on the specific player with the ball and the players in the immediate vicinity of the ball.

R: C.   Initial keys for the R include the player(s) in position to receive the snap and blockers in the backfield.

LJ: D.   Initial keys for the LJ include the snapper, all players lined up on their respective line of scrimmage, and wide receivers on the LJ side of the snapper.

BJ: E.   Initial keys for the BJ are all wide receivers on the BJ side of the snapper.

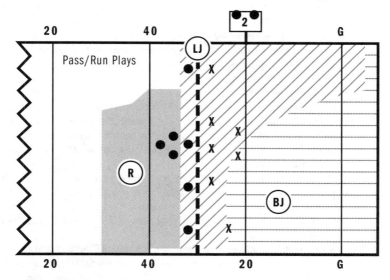

Article 3. Running and Passing Play Coverage.

All: A.   Flag football is primarily a passing game. However, officials must also be prepared for designed runs and runs that develop out of passing formations. Backward passes are also a staple of the game, so all officials must be prepared to accurately rule on the direction of a pass anywhere on the field. Always box-in the play. Avoid situations that may cause scrambling to avoid interference with players. Stay wide. It is always easier to move in than back out.

R: B. **The R's mental checklist is: Snap, Ball, QB, Rush, and Pass.** Be ready to rule the snap dead if it strikes the ground prior to being possessed. After the snap, observe the action behind the neutral zone, focusing on the quarterback and blockers surrounding the QB or runner. Adjust your position to see through the play and maintain an "inside-out" look, which keeps the action in between you and the sideline. Mark forward progress if it ends behind the line of scrimmage. Assist the BJ with the runner who goes out of bounds on your sideline near the line of scrimmage or in the backfield. Once the runner advances downfield, remain near the neutral zone and officiate the play from behind, keeping all players in front of you.

R: C. Remain wider and deeper than the passer, and be aware of a potential backward pass to another passer. Unless the pass is thrown immediately at the snap, you are responsible for ruling on the direction of all passes behind the line of scrimmage. If in doubt, the pass is backward. When the forward pass is thrown, announce "ball's away" and keep your vision on the passer until there is no threat of a foul. You are primarily responsible for Roughing the Passer and Intentional Grounding. If a forward pass is thrown near the A scrimmage line, hustle to the spot of the throw and check the legality of the pass. If in doubt, the pass is legal.

LJ: D. **The LJ's mental checklist is: Snap, Keys, Zone, and Ball.** After the snap, hold your position for a second to observe the initial charge of the line players and rule on any immediate contact created by either team. Read the movements of your initial keys. If you read run, hold at the neutral zone and observe the screen blockers and defenders ahead of and around the runner. If a pass is thrown immediately at the snap, rule on the direction of the pass. If you read pass, slide downfield 3 to 5 yards and observe the middle of field, along with receivers who threaten the sideline. Be alert for the QB becoming a runner near the sideline. Once the forward pass is thrown, move to a position to see between the receiver and the defender. Maintain an "outside-in" look, which keeps the action in between you and the middle of the field.

LJ: E. As the runner advances beyond the neutral zone, keep a position that is parallel to the runner and rule on the legality of all backward passes beyond the line of scrimmage. Mark forward progress from the neutral zone to approximately 20 yards downfield. You are primarily responsible for ruling on the line-to-gain and solely responsible for your sideline from end line to end line.

BJ: F. **The BJ's mental checklist is: Snap, Keys, Zone, and Ball.** After the snap, hold your position for a second to observe the initial movements of your initial keys. If you read run, watch the screen blockers ahead of and around the runner. If the runner moves toward your sideline, move to the sideline and maintain an "outside-in" look. If you read pass, move backward as the receivers establish their patterns. Let the play come to you but do not allow any players to get behind you. Once the forward pass is thrown, move to a position to see between the receiver and the defender.

BJ: G. As the runner advances beyond the neutral zone, lead the play toward the goal line while observing the blockers surrounding and ahead of the runner. On long scoring plays, stand still on the goal line when the runner crosses. On long passing plays that threaten the end line, move off of the goal line to cover the end line. You are primarily responsible for your sideline beyond the neutral zone, the goal line on long plays, and the end line.

Article 4. Line-to-Gain Coverage on 3rd and 4th Down.

R: A.   Your initial position, keys, and coverage responsibilities remain the same as standard scrimmage plays.

LJ: B.   Your initial position and keys remain the same as standard scrimmage plays. If the ball is snapped 10 yards or less from the line-to-gain, hustle to the line-to-gain immediately following the snap. Hold your position on the line-to-gain and rule on either a 1st down or forward progress short of the line-to-gain. Do not leave the line-to-gain until either the runner is clearly beyond the line-to-gain or the ball becomes dead by rule.

BJ: C.   Your initial position, keys, and coverage responsibilities remain the same as standard scrimmage plays.

Article 5. Goal Line and Try Coverage.

R: A.   Your initial position, keys, and coverage responsibilities remain the same as standard scrimmage plays.

LJ: B.   Your initial position and keys remain the same as standard scrimmage plays. If the ball is snapped on or inside B's 10 yard line, hustle to the goal line immediately following the snap. Hold your position on the goal line and rule on either a touchdown or forward progress short of the goal line.

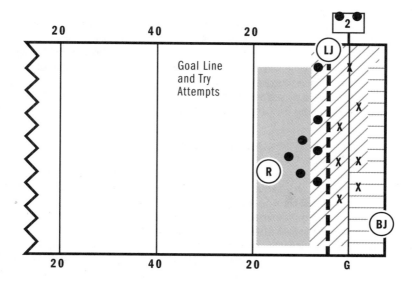

Goal Line and Try Attempts

BJ: C.   Your initial position, keys, and coverage responsibilities remain the same as standard scrimmage plays. If the ball is snapped on or inside B's 10 yard line, start on the end line, 5 yards from your sideline. Do not leave the end line until the ball becomes dead by rule or there is a change of possession.

Article 6. Reverse Mechanics.

All: A.   Reverse mechanics apply to situations following a change of team possession.

R: B.   Following a change of possession, R coverage responsibilities become similar to those of the BJ. Lead the play toward the goal line while observing the blockers surrounding and ahead of the runner. Stand still on the goal line when the runner crosses.

LJ: C.   Following a change of possession, LJ coverage responsibilities remain the same.

BJ: D.   Following a change of possession, BJ coverage responsibilities become similar to those of the R. As the runner advances, officiate the play from behind, keeping all players in front of you. Maintain responsibility for your sideline. If appropriate, pick up the ball spotters and return them to the R at the end of the play.

Article 7. Reverse Goal Line Mechanics.

All: A.   Reverse goal line mechanics apply to situations where A snaps the ball close to their own goal line.

R: B.   If the offensive formation forces your initial 7×7 position to be on or inside the goal line, start on the goal line and be wider than usual to keep an appropriate angle. Take responsibility for the goal line and the end line, ruling on either a safety or forward progress in advance of the goal line.

R: C.   If the ball is snapped on or inside A's 10 yard line, start on the end line. Do not leave the end line until the goal line is no longer threatened and the play has moved downfield.

LJ: D.   If the ball is snapped on or inside A's 10 yard line, hustle to the goal line immediately following the snap. Stay on the goal line and rule on either a safety or forward progress in advance of the goal line. Do not leave the goal line until it is no longer threatened and the play has moved downfield.

BJ: E.   If the ball is snapped on or inside A's 10 yard line, the LJ will be occupied with the goal line, so expand your coverage area and be prepared to help in zones typically covered by the LJ.

Section 2. Punt Plays

Article 1. Before the Snap.

R: A.   Prior to all 4th down plays, ask the coach or captain if A wants to punt. Communicate this decision to all players and coaches, and then mark the ball ready for play. Inform both teams to stay out of the neutral zone until the ball is punted.

R: B.   Your initial position remains the same as standard scrimmage plays.

LJ: C.   Your initial position remains the same as standard scrimmage plays.

BJ: D.   Take an initial position on the opposite side of the field as the LJ. Start approximately 3 yards behind the deepest receiver and at least 10 yards wide of the nearest receiver. If the deepest receiver lines up on or inside R's 10 yard line, stand on the goal line and be wider than usual to keep an appropriate angle.

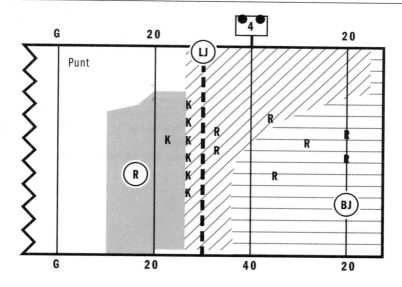

Article 2. Reading and Understanding Keys.

R: A.   Your initial keys remain the same as standard scrimmage plays.

LJ: B.   Your initial keys remain the same as standard scrimmage plays.

BJ: C.   Your initial keys are the deepest R players in position to receive the kick.

Article 3. Punt Coverage.

All: A.   Once the punt is caught, utilize reverse mechanics.

R: B.   Watch for the snap hitting the ground and the kicker punting the ball. If the punt goes out of bounds in flight, line up the wing official by chopping your arm (S1) as they reach the out-of-bounds spot.

LJ: C.   After the snap, rule on any scrimmage line fouls and hold your position until the ball crosses K's scrimmage line. If the ball is kicked short, take responsibility for the receiver and drop the bean bag where the kick ends. As the ball is in the air, move downfield in front of the runner, observing blockers in front of the runner. Once the runner catches up to you, officiate the play as normal.

BJ: D.   After the snap, work to maintain a 45 degree angle with the receiver while the ball is in flight. Once the ball is caught, drop the bean bag where the kick ends, and observe the blockers around the runner. You are responsible for R's goal line. If the punt lands or rolls near the goal line, stay wide and straddle the goal line, ruling on touchbacks.

LJ, BJ: E.   If punted out of bounds on the ground on your sideline, mark the spot. If punted out of bounds in the air, jog to the approximate area, then begin walking slowly until the R chops you in (S1) to mark the spot.

Section 3. Co-Rec Adjustments

Article 1. Scrimmage Play Coverage.

All: A.   Verify the open/closed status with other officials prior to the R marking the ball ready for play.

R: B.   Announce open/closed status when marking the ball ready for play. Your initial position, keys, and coverage responsibilities remain the same as standard scrimmage plays. Rule on illegal reception, a 2nd forward pass thrown from behind the line of scrimmage, and whether the passer is behind or beyond A's scrimmage line when the pass is thrown.

LJ: C.   Your initial position, keys, and coverage responsibilities remain the same as standard scrimmage plays. Rule on illegal advancement.

BJ: D.   Your initial position, keys, and coverage responsibilities remain the same as standard scrimmage plays.

PART VI. 4-PERSON MECHANICS

Section 1. Scrimmage Plays

Article 1. Before the Snap.

All: A. Initial positions may vary depending upon play situations, team formations, tendencies, field, and weather conditions. Always box in the play, as all players should be in the collective vision of the officiating crew at all times. When in doubt, take a position that is wider and deeper that avoids interfering with the players.

All: B. Signal and verify the down with other officials. Check the down box for accuracy. Communicate the clock status as necessary. Remind the players to tuck in their jerseys and adjust their flag belts as necessary. Be alert for time-outs, dead ball fouls, injuries, and anything out of the ordinary. Ensure that all officials are in proper position prior to allowing the ball to become live.

R: C. Take an initial position on the opposite side of the field as the LJ and on the same side as the FJ. Start approximately 7 yards behind and 7 yards wide of the deepest offensive back at a 45 degree angle. Be in a position to see the snap, backs, and players near the snapper. Be alert for false starts and illegal shifts by A. Communicate to A when there are 15 seconds and 10 seconds remaining on the play clock. With 5 seconds remaining on the play clock, count down 5-4-3-2-1 so that the player(s) in position to receive the snap can hear.

R: D. Upon the conclusion of the previous play, set the ball spotters in the appropriate location on or inside the hash marks to create the neutral zone. Announce the down/distance and mark the ball ready for play by blowing your whistle and giving the appropriate signal (S1). The ready for play procedure and announcement should not prevent a team from snapping the ball quickly. Start timing the play clock upon marking the ball ready for play. Announce "Double Stakes" if A must obtain two lines-to-gain, and "Triple Stakes" for three lines-to-gain.

LJ: E. Take an initial position between the neutral zone on the sideline opposite the R and FJ. If wide receivers line up near the sideline, or if the line-to-gain or goal line is threatened, start 2 yards off the sideline. Be in a position to see the snap, neutral zone, and players on both sides of the line of scrimmage. Be aware of incoming and exiting substitutes. Be alert for encroachments, false starts, illegal snaps, illegal formations, illegal shifts, and illegal motions. Take responsibility for A players in motion at the snap.

LJ: F. Upon the conclusion of the previous play, mark the forward progress spot and indicate the next location of the A scrimmage line. Use your downfield foot and raise your arm straight above your head while indicating the next down. Upon giving the R the spot, communicate the next down and distance to the down box.

FJ: G. Take an initial position on the sideline opposite of the LJ. If wide receivers line up near the sideline, or if the line-to-gain or goal line is threatened, start 2 yards off the sideline. Start 10 yards beyond A's scrimmage line. Line up at a 45 degree angle to the sideline. Be aware of incoming and exiting substitutes.

FJ: H. Upon the conclusion of the previous play, if necessary, mark the forward progress spot and pass this spot onto the LJ to indicate the next location of the A scrimmage line.

BJ:	I.	Take an initial position on the same side of the field as the LJ, opposite of the R. Start approximately 20 yards beyond A's scrimmage line, always deeper than the deepest defensive back, and 15 yards from the sideline on the hash mark. Communicate the clock status as necessary.
BJ:	J.	Upon the conclusion of the previous play, if necessary, mark the forward progress spot and pass this spot onto the LJ to indicate the next location of the A scrimmage line.

Article 2. Reading and Understanding Keys.

All:	A.	Keys are intended to help determine officials' coverage areas at the initial snap. Officials must be prepared to react to the play as it develops. Keys do not necessarily determine coverage for the entire play, as constant adjustments are necessary.
All:	B.	Officials should become familiar with the concept of "player, zone, ball." Player refers to the initial key(s) that the official should focus on at the snap. As the play develops, officials should switch to covering a zone of the field that could impact the play. Once the offense commits to passing or running into a specific zone, covering officials should focus their attention on the specific player with the ball and the players in the immediate vicinity of the ball.
R:	C.	Initial keys for the R include the player(s) in position to receive the snap and blockers in the backfield.
LJ:	D.	Initial keys for the LJ include the snapper and blockers lined up in the immediate vicinity of the snapper.
FJ:	E.	Initial keys for the FJ are all wide receivers on the FJ side of the snapper.
BJ:	F.	Initial keys for the BJ are all wide receivers on the LJ side of the snapper.

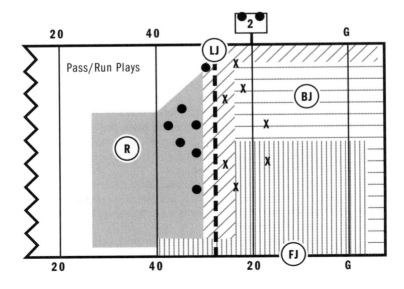

Article 3. Running and Passing Play Coverage.

All: A.   Flag football is primarily a passing game. However, officials must also be prepared for designed runs and runs that develop out of a passing formation. Backward passes are also a staple of the game, so all officials must be prepared to accurately rule on the direction of a pass anywhere on the field. Always box-in the play. Avoid situations that may cause scrambling to avoid interference with players. Stay wide. It is always easier to move in than back out.

R: B.   **The R's mental checklist is: Snap, Ball, QB, Rush, and Pass.** Be ready to rule the snap dead if it strikes the ground prior to being possessed. After the snap, observe the action behind the neutral zone, focusing on the quarterback and blockers surrounding the QB or runner. Adjust your position to see through the play and maintain an "inside-out" look, which keeps the action in between you and the sideline. Mark forward progress if it ends behind the line of scrimmage. Assist the FJ with the runner who goes out of bounds on your sideline near the line of scrimmage or in the backfield. Once the runner advances downfield, remain near the neutral zone and officiate the play from behind, keeping all players in front of you.

R: C.   Remain wider and deeper than the passer, and be aware of a potential backward pass to another passer. Unless the pass is thrown immediately at the snap, you are responsible for ruling on the direction of all passes behind the line of scrimmage. If in doubt, the pass is backward. When the forward pass is thrown, announce "ball's away" and keep your vision on the passer until there is no threat of a foul. You are primarily responsible for Roughing the Passer and Intentional Grounding. If a forward pass is thrown near the A scrimmage line, hustle to the spot of the throw and check the legality of the pass. If in doubt, the pass is legal.

LJ: D.   **The LJ's mental checklist is: Snap, Keys, Zone, and Ball.** After the snap, hold your position for a second to observe the initial charge of the line players and rule on any immediate contact created by either team. Read the movements of your initial keys. If you read run, hold at the neutral zone and observe the screen blockers and defenders ahead of and around the runner. If a pass is thrown immediately at the snap, rule on the direction of the pass. If you read pass, slide downfield 3 to 5 yards and observe the middle of field, along with receivers who threaten the sideline. Be alert for the QB becoming a runner near your sideline. Once the forward pass is thrown, move to a position to see between the receiver and the defender. Maintain an "outside-in" look, which keeps the action in between you and the middle of the field.

LJ: E.   As the runner advances beyond the neutral zone, keep a position that is parallel to the runner and rule on the legality of backward passes beyond the line of scrimmage. Take responsibility for your sideline from end line to end line. You are primarily responsible for forward progress, unless the runner goes out of bounds on the opposite sideline. Be prepared to defer the forward progress spot to the FJ or BJ on long plays downfield.

FJ: F.   **The FJ's mental checklist is: Snap, Keys, Zone, and Ball.** After the snap, hold your position for a second to observe the initial movements of your initial keys. If you read run, watch the screen blockers ahead of and around the runner. If you read pass, move backward as the receivers establish their patterns. Be alert for the QB becoming a runner on your sideline.

Once the forward pass is thrown, move to a position to see between the receiver and the defender. Maintain an "outside-in" look, which keeps the action in between you and the middle of the field.

FJ: G.   As the runner advances beyond the neutral zone, stay ahead of the play and lead it to the goal line. Take responsibility for your sideline from end line to end line. When the runner goes out of bounds, blow your whistle, mark the forward progress spot, and pass it off to the LJ. Be prepared to assist the LJ with marking forward progress on long plays.

BJ: H.   **The BJ's mental checklist is: Snap, Keys, Zone, and Ball.** After the snap, hold your position for a second to observe the initial movements of the A players. If you read run, watch the screen blockers ahead of and around the runner. Adjust your position to see through the play and maintain an "inside-out" look, which keeps the action in between you and the sideline. If you read pass, move backward as the receivers establish their patterns. Let the play come to you but do not allow any players to get behind you. Once the forward pass is thrown, move to a position to see between the receiver and the defender.

BJ: I.   As the runner advances beyond the neutral zone, lead the play toward the goal line while observing the blockers surrounding and ahead of the runner. On long scoring plays, stand still on the goal line when the runner crosses. On long passing plays that threaten the end line, move off of the goal line to cover the end line. You are primarily responsible for the goal line on long plays, and solely responsible for B's end line. Be prepared to assist the LJ or FJ with marking forward progress on long plays.

Article 4. Line-to-Gain Coverage on 3rd and 4th Down.

R: A.   Your initial position, keys, and coverage responsibilities remain the same as standard scrimmage plays.

LJ: B.   Your initial position and keys remain the same as standard scrimmage plays. If the ball is snapped 3 yards or less from the line-to-gain, hustle to the line-to-gain immediately following the snap. Do not leave the line-to-gain until either the runner is clearly beyond the line-to-gain or the ball becomes dead by rule. You are primarily responsible for determining if the line-to-gain was achieved. Defer to the FJ if the play ends near the intersection of the opposite sideline and the line-to-gain.

LJ: C.   If the ball is snapped more than 3 yards from the line-to-gain, the FJ is primarily responsible for determining if the line-to-gain was achieved. If your normal coverage of the play takes you to the line-to-gain, stop there. Do not leave the line-to-gain until either the runner is clearly beyond the line-to-gain or the ball becomes dead by rule. You should assist the FJ if the play ends near the intersection of your sideline and the line-to-gain.

FJ: D.   If the ball is snapped 3 yards or less from the line-to-gain, your initial position remains the same as standard scrimmage plays. The LJ is primarily responsible for determining if the line-to-gain was achieved. You should assist the LJ if the play ends near the intersection of your sideline and the line-to-gain.

FJ: E.   If the ball is snapped more than 14 yards from the line-to-gain, your initial position remains the same as standard scrimmage plays. If your normal coverage of the play takes you to the line-to-gain, stop there. Do not leave the line-to-gain until either the runner is clearly beyond the line-to-gain or the ball becomes dead by rule.

FJ: F.   If the ball is snapped more than 3 yards but not more than 14 yards from the line-to-gain, your initial position is the line-to-gain. Hold your position on the line-to-gain and rule on either a 1st down or forward progress short of the line-to-gain. You are primarily responsible for determining if the line-to-gain was achieved. Defer to the LJ if the play ends near the intersection of the opposite sideline and the line-to-gain.

BJ: G.   Your initial position, keys, and coverage responsibilities remain the same as standard scrimmage plays.

Article 5. Goal Line and Try Coverage.

R: A.   Your initial position, keys, and coverage responsibilities remain the same as standard scrimmage plays.

LJ: B.   Your initial position and keys remain the same as standard scrimmage plays. If the ball is snapped 5 yards or less from B's goal line, hustle to the goal line immediately following the snap. Hold your position on the goal line and rule on either a touchdown or forward progress short of the goal line. You should assist the FJ if the play ends near the intersection of your sideline and the goal line. Be prepared to communicate with the BJ on potential catches near the intersection of your sideline and the end line.

FJ: C.   If the ball is snapped on or inside B's 14 yard line, your initial position is the goal line. Hold your position on the goal line and rule on either a touchdown or forward progress short of the goal line. You are primarily responsible for determining if the runner crosses the goal line. Defer to the LJ if the play ends near the intersection of the opposite sideline and the goal line. Be prepared to communicate with the BJ on potential catches near the intersection of your sideline and the end line.

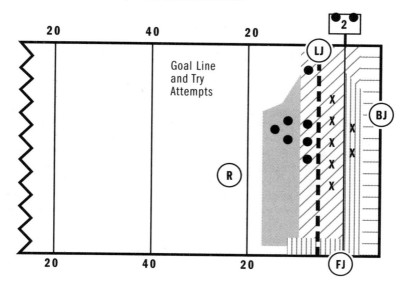

FJ: D.   If the ball is snapped more than 14 yards from B's goal line, your initial position remains the same as standard scrimmage plays.

BJ: E.   If the ball is snapped on or inside B's 14 yard line, start on the end line. Do not leave the end line until the ball becomes dead by rule or there is a change of possession. Be prepared to communicate with the LJ or the FJ on potential catches near the intersection of a sideline and the end line.

Article 6. Reverse Mechanics.

All: A.   Reverse mechanics apply to situations following a change of team possession.

R: B.   Following a change of possession, R coverage responsibilities become similar to those of the BJ. Lead the play toward the goal line while observing the blockers surrounding and ahead of the runner. You should be positioned stationary on the goal line when the runner crosses.

LJ: C.   Following a change of possession, LJ coverage responsibilities become similar to those of the FJ. Lead the play toward the goal line while observing the blockers surrounding and ahead of the runner.

FJ: D.   Following a change of possession, FJ coverage responsibilities become similar to those of the LJ. Keep a position that is parallel to the runner, ruling on the legality of backward passes. You are primarily responsible for forward progress.

BJ: E.   Following a change of possession, BJ coverage responsibilities become similar to those of the R. As the runner advances, officiate the play from behind, keeping all players in front of you. If appropriate, pick up the ball spotters and return them to the R at the end of the play.

Article 7. Reverse Goal Line Mechanics.

All: A.   Reverse goal line mechanics apply to situations where A snaps the ball close to their own goal line.

R: B.   If the offensive formation forces your initial 7×7 position to be on or inside the goal line, start on the goal line and be wider than usual to keep an appropriate angle. Take responsibility for the goal line and the end line, ruling on either a safety or forward progress in advance of the goal line.

R: C.   If the ball is snapped on or inside A's 10 yard line, start on the end line. Do not leave the end line until the goal line is no longer threatened and the play has moved downfield.

LJ: D.   If the ball is snapped on or inside A's 10 yard line, hustle to the goal line immediately following the snap. Hold your position on the goal line and rule on either a safety or forward progress in advance of the goal line. Do not leave the goal line until it is no longer threatened and the play has moved downfield.

FJ: E.   If the ball is snapped on or inside A's 10 yard line, the LJ will be occupied with the goal line, so expand your coverage area and be prepared to help in zones typically covered by the LJ.

BJ: F.   If the ball is snapped on or inside A's 10 yard line, your initial position and coverage responsibilities remain the same as standard scrimmage plays.

Section 2. Punt Plays

Article 1. Before the Snap.

R: A.   Prior to all 4th down plays, ask the coach or captain if A wants to punt. Communicate this decision to all players and coaches. Inform both teams to stay out of the neutral zone until the ball is punted.

R: B.   Your initial position remains the same as standard scrimmage plays.

LJ: C.   Your initial position remains the same as standard scrimmage plays.

FJ: D.   Take an initial position on your sideline approximately 5 yards ahead of the deepest receiver.

BJ: E.   Take an initial position on the same side of the field as the LJ. Start approximately 3 yards behind the deepest receiver and at least 8 yards wide of the nearest receiver. If the deepest receiver lines up on or inside R's 10 yard line, stand on the goal line and be wider than usual to keep an appropriate angle.

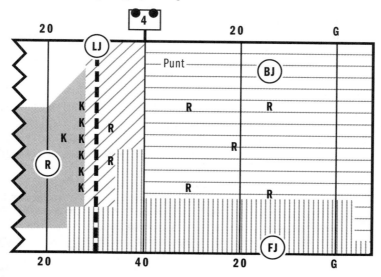

Article 2. Reading and Understanding Keys.

R: A.   Your initial keys remain the same as standard scrimmage plays.

LJ: B.   Your initial keys remain the same as standard scrimmage plays.

FJ: C.   Your initial keys remain the same as standard scrimmage plays.

BJ: D.   Your initial keys are the deepest R players in position to receive the kick.

Article 3. Punt Coverage.

All: A.   Once the punt is caught, utilize reverse mechanics.

R: B.   Watch for the snap hitting the ground and the kicker punting the ball. If the punt goes out of bounds in flight, line up the wing official by chopping your arm (S1) as they reach the out-of-bounds spot.

LJ: C.   After the snap, rule on any scrimmage line fouls and hold your position until the ball crosses K's scrimmage line. If the ball is kicked short and near your sideline, take responsibility for the receiver and drop the bean bag where the kick ends. As the ball is in the air, move downfield in front of the runner, observing blockers in front of the runner. Once the runner catches up to you, officiate the play as normal.

FJ: D.   If the ball is kicked short and near your sideline, take responsibility for the receiver and drop the bean bag where the kick ends. During the kick, observe blockers in front of the runner, allowing the BJ to be responsible for the receivers. Once the ball is caught, take responsibility for the runner and forward progress.

LJ, FJ: E.   If punted out of bounds on the ground on your sideline, mark the spot. If punted out of bounds in the air, jog to the approximate area, then begin walking slowly until the R chops you in (S1) to mark the spot.

BJ: F.   After the snap, work to maintain a 45 degree angle with the receiver while the ball is in flight. Once the ball is caught, drop the bean bag where the kick ends, and observe the blockers around the runner. You are responsible for R players' goal line. If the punt lands or rolls near the goal line, stay wide and straddle the goal line, ruling on touchbacks.

Section 3. Co-Rec Adjustments

Article 1. Scrimmage Play Coverage.

All: A.   Verify the open/closed status with other officials prior to the R marking the ball ready for play.

R: B.   Announce open/closed status when marking the ball ready for play. Your initial position, keys, and coverage responsibilities remain the same as standard scrimmage plays. Rule on illegal reception, a 2nd forward pass thrown from behind the line of scrimmage, and whether the passer is behind or beyond A's scrimmage line when the pass is thrown.

LJ: C.   Your initial position, keys, and coverage responsibilities remain the same as standard scrimmage plays. Rule on illegal advancement.

FJ: D.   Your initial position, keys, and coverage responsibilities remain the same as standard scrimmage plays.

BJ: E.   Your initial position, keys, and coverage responsibilities remain the same as standard scrimmage plays.

PART VII. NIRSA OFFICIAL FLAG FOOTBALL SIGNALS

NIRSA Official Flag Football Signals

Ball ready for play
(1B Untimed down)

Start clock

Time-out Discretionary or injury time-out
(followed by tapping hands on chest)

Touchdown,
point(s) after
touchdown

Safety

Dead ball foul
Touchback
(move side to side)

First down

Loss of down

Incomplete forward
pass, Penalty
declined, No play,
no score, Toss
option deferred

Legal touching of
forward pass or
scrimmage kick

Inadvertent whistle

Disregard flag

End of period

Sideline warning

First touching

Backward pass

Encroachment

False start
Illegal formation
Illegal procedure
Illegal advancement
Illegal reception

Illegal shift
(2 hands)
Illegal motion
(1 hand)

Delay of game

Substitution
infraction

Failure to wear required
equipment/Disconcerting act

Flag guarding

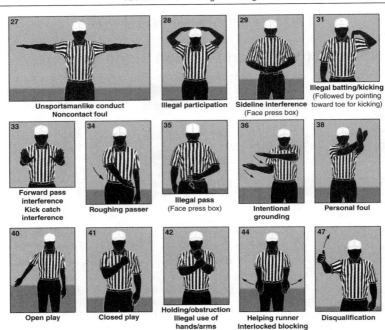

27	**28**	**29**	**31**
			Illegal batting/kicking (Followed by pointing toward toe for kicking)
Unsportsmanlike conduct **Noncontact foul**	**Illegal participation**	**Sideline interference** (Face press box)	
33	**34**	**35**	**36**	**38**
Forward pass interference **Kick catch interference**	**Roughing passer**	**Illegal pass** (Face press box)	**Intentional grounding**	**Personal foul**
40	**41**	**42**	**44**	**47**
Open play	**Closed play**	**Holding/obstruction** **Illegal use of hands/arms**	**Helping runner** **Interlocked blocking**	**Disqualification**

PlayPic® PlayPics courtesy of **REFEREE** (www.referee.com)

Missing signal numbers are intended for future expansion.

INDEX TO RULES